Out There

In the Wild in a Wired Age

TED KERASOTE

Voyageur Press

SA PL

Edited by Josh Leventhal
Designed by Maria Friedrich
Printed in China

04   05   06   07   08   5   4   3   2   1

Library of Congress Cataloging-in-Publication Data

Kerasote, Ted.
Out there : in the wild in a wired age / by Ted Kerasote.
p. cm.
ISBN 0-89658-556-5 (hardcover)
1. Kerasote, Ted—Journeys—Northwest, Canadian.
2. Canoeists—United States—Biography. I. Title.
GV782.42.K45A3 2004
797.1'22'092—dc22

2003022800

Published by Voyageur Press, Inc.
123 North Second Street, P.O. Box 338,
Stillwater, MN 55082 U.S.A.
651-430-2210, fax 651-430-2211
books@voyageurpress.com
www.voyageurpress.com

*Educators, fundraisers, premium and gift buyers, publicists, and
marketing managers:* Looking for creative products and new sales ideas?
Voyageur Press books are available at special discounts when purchased
in quantities, and special editions can be created to your specifi-
cations. For details contact the marketing department at 800-888-9653.

CONTENTS

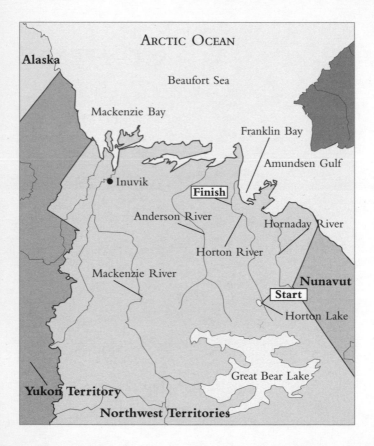

ARCTIC OCEAN

Alaska

Beaufort Sea

Mackenzie Bay

Franklin Bay

Amundsen Gulf

• Inuvik

Finish

Anderson River

Hornaday River

Horton River

Mackenzie River

Nunavut

Start

Horton Lake

Great Bear Lake

Yukon Territory

Northwest Territories

EMPTINESS

The Horton River heads on a rise of barren land north of Great Bear Lake in the far northwest corner of Canada's Northwest Territories. It flows west and north and west and north again, some 400 miles, before winding through a range of smoking hills and emptying into the Arctic Ocean. It's one of the remoter spots on Earth. Protected by great distances from populated areas, an inhospitable climate, and a lack of precious metals, oil, and gas, it has remained much as it was when the Laurentide ice sheet melted away 7,000 years ago: the home of grizzly bears, caribou, musk ox, eagles, and an infinity of space. Even Eskimos living relatively close by on the coast never made any permanent settlements in the Horton Valley, traversing it only intermittently while on summer caribou hunts.

In a noisy age, it seemed like the perfect place to go for a vacation.

We leave Inuvik, on the Mackenzie River Delta, at

about five o'clock on an August afternoon, climbing sky-ward in a Cessna 185, chock-full of three weeks worth of food, camping gear, and our folding canoe. Inuvik—a few gravel streets, homes on stilts because of the permafrost, and a long runway for jets—shrinks into the pastel green tundra behind us. From horizon to horizon, the only other sign that people have been this way is the threadlike line of the Dempster Highway, snaking its rutted way 800 miles south to Whitehorse in the Yukon Territory.

Four hundred miles west of the Dempster is another road, the Dalton Highway, connecting the oil field at Prudhoe Bay to Fairbanks, Alaska. As in the case of the Dempster, "highway" should be understood in the loosest of terms: gravel, potholes, frost heaves, no center line, few services. To the east there are no roads at all. In fact, we would have to fly across the entirety of Canada, the Davis Strait, Greenland, and the Norwegian Sea before crossing the next road, on the coast of Scandinavia. Likewise, to the north we'd have to fly over the pole, across the Laptev Sea, and about 600 miles farther south into Siberia before reaching the first road on the other side of the globe. In short, we're flying into the largest ice-free roadless area on the planet, dotted by a handful of native settlements and the occasional cut of an old seismic line, now growing over with tundra and willow but still visible from the air. In the sky overhead there isn't even a contrail—no international jet routes cross this rarely visited corner of the north.

The other half of the "we" embarking on this canoe trip is Len Carlman, my longtime friend, attorney, and father of my godson. Len reminds me of the descriptions I've read of the young Dick Cheney: serious, methodical, and thoughtful to a fault. However, Len's politics are nothing like the former oil man's. In his twenties and early thirties, Len was the head of one of Wyoming's larger conservation organizations, working to protect open space and wilderness areas. This trip to the far north, his first, is a pilgrimage to holy ground, one that makes our homeplace of Yellowstone (often billed as one of the least developed regions of the Lower 48) seem civilized.

Fortunately, Len knows how to lighten his encyclopedic knowledge of politics and his unremitting civic-mindedness (he volunteers regularly for local causes) with a healthy dose of elfish humor. He has a shock of short red hair, dancing blue eyes, and a whooping laugh that reveals a childlike wonder at moments many adults might find ordinary: camping in the backyard with his children, building them an igloo playhouse, and fiddling with his ever-present Palm Pilot, onto which he has downloaded six novels to read during the inevitable storm days we'll encounter. He now sleeps in the rear seat of the 185, exhausted from finishing his case load before our departure, as well as fulfilling his ongoing fatherly duties: Len's one-year-old son still keeps him and his wife, Anne, up for parts of many a night.

The plane drones. Our pilot, Corey—a tall, pleasant, loose-jointed wildlife biologist from Saskatchewan who spends his summers flying in the Arctic—keeps his hands on the yoke and his eyes on the sky. To the southwest, the sun lowers in a China-blue heaven, but darkness won't overtake us today nor tomorrow nor any day of this trip. Circling to the north, the sun will skim the ice-capped ocean, and climb into the northeast to begin another dawn. For me the endless light is welcome. Without the daily round of sunrise and sunset, our most ingrained of quotidian routines can be broken, allowing us to enter other rhythms. Len and I can paddle until midnight, dine at 2:00 A.M., sleep until 11:00, and begin another stretch of river after a leisurely brunch.

I have longed for this change in schedule, for during the past seven months I completed an anthology of wilderness essays under a very tight schedule—writing the book's introduction and editing a dozen contributions, while also coordinating with a GIS mapping firm, the editor of the publishing house, the designer, copyeditor, fact checker, and the institution that provided the funding. It was by no means difficult physical work, but it had its challenges, especially for a person accustomed to spending so much time outdoors. I had to sit at my desk for seven to twelve hours each day, communicating by phone and e-mail with the entire team, many of whom worked as far apart as Washington State and Washington, D.C. Routinely, half a dozen people had to sign off on each phase of the project.

My little office in Wyoming felt abuzz with electronic energy, sometimes two different phones and the fax machine ringing simultaneously while the designer and I, a thousand miles apart, adjusted the book's layout on our respective computer monitors. In the best modern tradition of multitasking, each of us on the project was also simultaneously working on at least two other projects. And because data can now be transmitted almost instantly, everyone involved with these various books, magazine articles, and lecture tours slid into the expectation that not only could megabytes of information be sent with a few keystrokes, but also that the words, photographs, and ideas represented by these electronic bundles could be created in ever-shorter amounts of time, perhaps even be created instantly, transforming a flash of inspiration into a finished product without any intervening work.

What increased was production; what decreased was reflection. It seemed that no one—editors, writers, photographers, graphic designers—could really say "please, can we slow down" without being seen as unpatriotic, a slacker, a whiner. If data can move this quickly, went the unstated question, why can't our brains? Few spoke of our souls, or more practically our digestions. There is a reason why the United States, with the largest GNP in the world, has the least time for lunch.

Sometimes I would look out the window above my computer, across the valley of Jackson Hole to the Tetons, and imagine the dense web of radio traffic arcing overhead, connecting us in virtual office space where billions of conversations were taking place, either vocally or by e-mail, between people who had never seen each other although they had worked together for months if not years. Many of them were in cubicles, high in buildings, the noise of city traffic floating up from below, their view a facade of windows and a sliver of sky. In the course of selling my words, I've visited such offices many times, always leaving secure in the knowledge that I was returning to quieter places with greater vistas.

But even these landscapes have changed. The Jackson Hole airport has become far busier with the roar of commercial and corporate jets and the military throb of scenic helicopter flights. As wildlife management has become increasingly mired in politics and litigation, more Game and Fish Department bush planes and helicopters go overhead on surveys, collecting data for Environmental Impact Statements. And the old park road, which I can see in the distance from my house, now bears a steadier stream of pickup trucks pulling all-terrain vehicles, as if a significant portion of our population is now afflicted with a paralytic disease and can no longer walk in the backcountry.

Even in the evening, when the workday was done and the air traffic quiet, the house remained filled with the ambient noise of what almost all of us have adopted as necessary technology: the electronic whispers and whines of refrigerator and freezer, and the subtle hum of the many devices standing at-ready—answering machines, stove and stereo clocks, smoke detectors. Most of us don't even notice this kind of low-grade static, for it has been with us since the day we were born, and in urban places it is overwhelmed by the noise of diesel engines, tire rumble, horns, sirens, subways, people moving on pavement. Only when we go to really quiet country do we notice how shocking silence can be, so thick away from the thrum of civilization that it presses against our flesh like the pressure beneath the sea.

Sometimes, when a heavy snowfall would temporarily stop electrical transmission to the entire valley, I would walk outside and stand under the inky blackness of the cleared night sky lights gone, the green transformer boxes, which sit astride each house and bring us power, mute. I would stand without moving and listen to the white noise of the nearby river grow apparent. Then, in a crossover of sensory perception that occurs only when diversions fall away, I could hear the stars sparkle. If the literal meaning of vacation is "freedom," then the Horton seemed about as free from technological overload as I would find without having to spend my holiday on one of the ice caps.

But we almost didn't make the trip.

Len couldn't be away from work for the full three weeks

that were needed to float the entire length of the river, with an additional two days of traveling on each end. With regrets, he begged off. I considered going alone—I've done long solo trips in the north before—but even with frequent phone and e-mail exchanges with colleagues and friends, I work by myself almost every day. On this trip, I wanted the physical company of an old companion; I wanted to share our mutual wonder at the river, the weather, the wildlife, and the sun circling round and round in the sky. In the end, the book project went on interminably, and I too couldn't leave early. I got back in touch with Len.

He was at his law office, and on the spur of the moment he called Anne, a sleek blond woman with a sharp sense of humor and a firm grasp on the value of leisure. He put the three of us on a conference line. Graciously, she encouraged him to go; teasingly, she also said that he'd pay big time, in terms of child care, when he got home. Len and I agreed to do the trip in two weeks, paddling extra-long days and taking out three-quarters of the way down the Horton if we were unable to reach the ocean. We would bring along an additional week of rations in the event we were stranded by weather.

Time being short, we met in town one afternoon, bought our food in two hours of shopping, packed it and our gear the next evening, and left a few days later, flying from Jackson Hole to Salt Lake City and then to Calgary, where we overnighted, and on to Inuvik, above the Arctic Circle, the following day. We changed clothes on the float plane's dock, crammed our gear into Corey's mothlike 185, and two-and-a-half hours later he spiraled down to Horton Lake, skimmed the surface, and left us on the beach—whisked from family, friends, radio, TV, e-mail, telephones, and traffic to willow, tundra, and sky just like that. The only vestige of the wired world we had left was the stipulation that Len's family had laid down for him, particularly his three sisters, who thought a grown man with two young children shouldn't be going off to run a grizzly-infested river in the Arctic. He was having a midlife crisis, one of them told me. Better, I responded, to go on a river trip with me than get a red Ferrari and a new blond.

They weren't mollified. If Len was going to accompany me to the Arctic, they said, he had to bring along a satellite phone—the kind that works anywhere in the world—in case of an emergency. After the recent media depictions of dramatic accidents involving experienced outdoor people in faraway places, I really couldn't say no to the phone, even though the subtext of bringing it along was apparent. It wouldn't only be used for an emergency; Len was expected to stay in touch. Networker and family man that he is, he thought it a fine idea.

2

PREDECESSORS

When John Franklin made his second expedition to the shores of the Polar Sea, looking for the Northwest Passage, he left England in February 1825, crossed the Atlantic Ocean, and arrived in New York City in March. He then went up the Hudson River to Albany, took coaches to Niagara Falls, sailed across Lake Ontario, and from there used carts, boats, and canoes to travel through the Great Lakes and on to Lake Winnipeg in present-day Saskatchewan. West and north he continued to Lake Athabasca, lying near the boundaries of what is today Alberta, Saskatchewan, and the Northwest Territories. Paddling and portaging his canoes, he made it to Great Slave Lake, where he entered the Mackenzie River and proceeded downstream 1,045 miles (according to his survey), before reaching the Arctic Ocean in August. The ocean would soon freeze, however, preventing any further explorations along the coast, so he turned around and made his way up the Mackenzie—no mean feat, as anyone that has paddled against the current to fetch a windblown sun hat knows.

As Franklin wrote, "[The] operations were tedious and hazardous. . . . The men had to walk with the towline along a narrow ledge that jutted out from the base of a steep rocky cliff, which was very slippery from the rain that had fallen in the night: a false step might have proved fatal; and we rejoiced when, having passed the rapids, we found earthy banks and a better path."

Franklin left the Mackenzie about two weeks later, ascended the Great Bear River, and entered Great Bear Lake, where he spent the winter, waiting for spring and ice-free conditions in the Arctic Ocean, to which he returned in July 1826 to begin his mapping. In other words, it was nearly a year and a half from the time he left England before he was in position to begin the job the British Admiralty had sent him out to do.

Splitting his party, Franklin went west toward Alaska, while Dr. John Richardson, the party's surgeon and naturalist, headed east along the Canadian coast. It was Richardson who, later in July, sailed by a range of "slate-clay" cliffs "six hundred feet high," through which a river debouched into a bay. He named the bay Franklin, after his commander, and the river itself after Wilmot Horton, Under Secretary of State for the Colonial Department. "Its breadth is about three hundred yards," Richardson wrote in his log, "and it seems, from the quantity of drift-timber that was piled on the shoals at its mouth, to flow through a wooded country." This observation was accurate: the Horton passes through the edge of North America's tree line, and in places, large and magnificent spruce, quite uncommon this far above the Arctic Circle, line its banks.

Richardson was on the quest for the Northwest Passage, the legendary channel that geographers believed would provide a commercial route between Europe and the riches of Asia, and so he coasted by the Horton without ascending it. He did, however, leave a black-and-white engraving, drawn by E. N. Kendall, one of the expedition's artists. It shows two tiny barks under reefed sails, passing beneath the mountains of the coast and between enormous piles of floating logs and icebergs. Overhead, unidentifiable and prehistoric-like birds soar. The scene has always reminded me of something out of Tolkien.

Proceeding some 500 miles to the east, Richardson continued to sprinkle the points, bays, and rivers of the Arctic shoreline with the names of his famous and forgotten colleagues: Point Deas Thompson, after John Deas Thompson, Esq., Commissioner of His Majesty's Navy;

Mount Hooker, for William Jackson Hooker, LL.D., Regius Professor of Botany at the University of Glasgow; Roscoe Bay, "after the eloquent historian of the Medici"; and Point De Witt Clinton, "as a testimony of our sense of the urbanity and love of science which had prompted his Excellency the Governor of the State of New York to show so much attention to the members of the Expedition, in their passage through his government."

Richardson then ascended the Coppermine River, first mapped in 1771 by the British explorer Samuel Hearne, when he came overland from Hudson Bay on an intrepid eighteen-month-long journey. Leaving the Coppermine, Richardson trekked to Great Bear Lake and was reunited with Franklin, who was to have met a British sailing ship in western Alaska, but, blocked by ice in that direction, had returned up the Mackenzie River. The expedition overwintered once again at the lake before retracing the long canoe, cart, and sea route back to England.

In the two men's jointly authored narrative—some 400 pages of prose, engravings, and tables of solar radiation, temperature, and latitude and longitude—there isn't a trace of wonder at the world through which they traveled. There is excitement about the utilitarian value of their discoveries to mankind, but there isn't the sense of awe that someone from today's era feels before raw and untouched nature.

Perhaps this is because there was so much nature then and so much less now: familiarity, if not breeding contempt, can produce complacency, and scarcity increases the value of everything from diamonds to empty space. One also has to consider that wonder had no place in the marching orders Franklin and Richardson received. They were to map unexplored coastlines and collect animal, plant, and mineral specimens. As Franklin wrote in the conclusion of his report, "Arctic discovery has been fostered principally by Great Britain; and it is a subject of just pride that it has been prosecuted by her from motives as disinterested as they are enlightened; not from any prospect of immediate benefit to herself, but from a steady view to the acquirement of useful knowledge, and the extension of the bounds of science." Both men were products of their century—rational, enlightened, dispassionate—and it would await a man of the next century to explore the country of the Horton with different motives.

That man was Vilhjalmur Stefansson, born in Canada of Icelandic parents and schooled in the United States. The north was in his genes and in his upbringing, and Harvard gave him a classical education. He made three long trips to the Arctic in the early 1900s—sledding, kayaking, eating caribou and seals, and living with and like the natives. A man of enormous fortitude and unsqueamish tastes (he often walked twenty miles over boggy tundra, pursuing game, and he declared three-year-old rotten whale meat palatable), Stefansson was also an ethnologist affiliated with the American Museum of Natural History. He found the Eskimos he lived with "agreeable" and declared them "not only interesting from a scientific point of view, as all primitive people must be to the student of mankind, but they were cheerful, self-reliant, and admirable companions."

Stefansson spent eleven years with them, in the prime of his life, traveling nomadically through Arctic Canada and Alaska as they did, and overwintering on the Horton, a place he called "the largest unexplored area on the continent." Like Franklin and Richardson before him, Stefansson was a scientist, loath to describe his emotions about country that was utterly unlike the familiar temperate world. In only one place in his Horton River account does he hint at what else might be going on for him besides writing a history of Arctic culture:

> Traveling at this time of year is particularly pleasant, for while the days are still warm, the placid nights are cool and the power of the mosquito has been broken. There are few things in one's experience in the North that are so pleasant to remember as these autumn hunts, when the camp is pitched among a clump of spruce

trees at the bottom of some ravine, and when at the end of a day's hunt you can gather around a crackling fire in the enveloping darkness, for the four-months' summer day is just over. The occasional howl of a wolf in the near shadow lends an additional romance, especially if, as not seldom happens, the wolves are so numerous and near that the dogs become frightened and gather in a close circle around the fire. . . . The dreams of boyhood seldom come true, but I am not sure that there is not sometimes as much romance about the reality of such evenings as there was about the dreams of Crusoe-like adventures on desert islands.

Despite such idyllic moments, Stefansson was also driven mad by the great loneliness he suffered in the Arctic, a back-and-forth tug he kept to his diary. "After the tent on the silent barrens," he wrote near the end of his Horton River trip, "I want Broadway by archlight and the Strand at five o'clock; after igloo I want the Century Club and the Criterion."

In the end, civilization won. Later in life, Stefansson settled in Greenwich Village, New York; Dearing Farm, Vermont; and Hanover, New Hampshire, where he devoted himself to his research library, collections, and the

Dartmouth College polar study program. As a sixty-two-year-old bachelor, he married Evelyn Baird, a dark-haired beauty far younger than he, who helped him with his writing, lecture tours, and growing notoriety—companions died on his later expeditions, his leadership was questioned, and he engaged in an ongoing dispute with Roald Amundsen, the first person to reach the South Pole and complete the Northwest Passage, about how to live well in the Arctic. If anything, Stefansson's fame increased. He wrote an Arctic survival manual for the U.S. Army during World War II, completed a treatise on diets in western civilization, and continued, until the very moment of his death at the age of eighty-three, to pump out books on the polar regions. While hosting a dinner party to celebrate the completion of his autobiography, Stefansson suffered a fatal stroke, with Evelyn at his side.

John Franklin knew no such marital happiness or sunset years of scholarship, but his life makes for a more mythic story. When he set off on his second polar expedition at the age of thirty-nine, he had been married for two years, and it was a lachrymose parting indeed. His wife, Eleanor, was dying, and in an act of selfless devotion she urged him to think of his duty rather than his love for her. He obeyed and left; she perished while he was gone.

Career-wise, setting off for the Arctic proved a good move. For mapping 1,200 miles of the Canadian coastline, Franklin was knighted, received an honorary degree from Oxford, and won a gold medal from the Geographical Society of Paris. He also didn't pine too long. In 1828 he remarried, going on to serve in the Mediterranean and as lieutenant-governor of Van Diemen's Land (now the Australian state of Tasmania). In May 1845, still tantalized by the discovery of the Northwest Passage, he returned to the Arctic a third time, once again leaving a wife behind.

His boats *Erebus* and *Terror* were last seen in July by a whaler at the entrance of Lancaster Sound, to the north of Baffin Island. Franklin then disappeared into the Arctic mists and not a word was heard from him for fourteen years. Starting in 1848, the first of more than forty search parties set sail, many of them funded by his wife, the stalwart Lady Jane, who divested herself of a fortune trying to discover what had happened to her husband. In the ensuing decade, a tremendous amount of geographical, biological, and ethnological information was collected as a byproduct of the search for Franklin and his crew. In 1859 Lady Jane received her answer. The captain of the *Fox*, a yacht she had purchased and outfitted, found abandoned equipment, skeletons, and a letter that told of the disaster: three hard winters, ships frozen in the ice, famine, cold, an overland journey hauling sleds and boats to no avail. The men fell in their tracks and died. Franklin had already expired, shortly before the summer solstice of 1847.

In a nation that lionized glorious failure as much as success, Sir John Franklin became a figure larger than life. And so did Lady Jane. Her story is as much a part of Arctic exploration as any man's, her name joined to her husband's on the monument erected to him in Westminster Abbey.

Nearly two centuries after Franklin sailed this coast, and nearly a hundred years after Stefansson sledded through this country, Len, married, and I, single, put on our bug jackets—nylon anoraks with mesh helmets that make us look like NASA astronauts. We walk through the dwarf willow to a point of land jutting into Horton Lake. The water flows by our feet and narrows into a creek that curves north and out of sight toward the main river and the Arctic Ocean, 400 miles away. The sky is a deep ambrosial blue, soft and inviting; there isn't a puff of wind; swarms of black-flies hover around our heads, stymied by the mesh and ny-lon. Unlike mosquitoes, they don't buzz.

Len asks me to stand by a rock at the very edge of the point so he can take my picture. I comply. The sun is warm, almost on the horizon, and casts marmalade light over the landscape. In the distance stretches a low range of hills. I smile—a compact man with dark eyes and chestnut hair— and the camera clicks. I ask Len to change places. He declines and instead asks me to take a picture of the lake after he throws a pebble into it. "Leave me out of the frame," he insists, and tosses the small stone. It makes an audible plop, and three perfect, enlarging rings spread across the surface of the water, whose blue is virtually indistinguishable from that of the sky. "Now," he says, and I trip the shutter. "That's the only picture I want of me," he adds.

3

SHOVING OFF

Compared to mountaineering trips, which have a sense of lean deprivation about them since every ounce of food, gear, and clothing must be carried on one's back, canoe journeys are lavish. Our particular folding canoe, sixteen and a half feet long, has a potential payload of 800 pounds. After subtracting Len's and my weight, 500 pounds of cargo space remain. That's a lot of tasty heavy food, extra clothing, and luxurious camping gear, like a solar shower, thick air mattresses, and folding chairs. However, if the river one is descending has rapids so large that they can't be run in an open canoe, as does the Horton, at some point one has to portage the boat and all the luxurious gear around them. Then one wishes one had been less indulgent.

Len and I have tried to balance our wish for comfort with easy portages and a fast-handling boat. Our entire pile of gear, including the canoe, weighs 285 pounds.

On a piece of high ground overlooking the lake, we erect the large blue tent, with its roomy vestibule, a sort of anteroom where one can hang wet gear, take off muddy boots, and even relieve oneself, if the weather is truly wretched. We then put up the extra mosquito netting, using canoe paddles as poles. Beneath it, we'll cook, for it's the wise camper in grizzly country who keeps food smells away from his or her sleeping quarters. In that vein, we also pile our food about a hundred yards from the blue tent—breakfasts, lunches, and dinners packed in cylinders of tough black plastic milled so smooth that a grizzly, or a person for that matter, has a hard time picking them up, much less prying off the seamlessly fitted lids. In treeless country, with no means to hang food out of the reach of bears, these containers can save both a trip and a bear's life, for faced with a bear ripping apart three weeks' worth of rations, many people, disliking the idea of starving, will fire a warning shot above the bear's head. Most bears will flee, but a few will charge, and the person wielding the shotgun or rifle—rightfully terrified—shoots the bear.

Neither Len nor I have any desire to kill a bear; hence the bear-proof food containers and two cans of pepper spray apiece. Filled with capsicum, the canisters shoot a cloud of orange spray to about forty feet. Several years of evidence from around North America has shown that a bear running into the capsicum cloud does an about-face. If you have had the wind change direction and received the cloud yourself, as I have had while testing the device, you immediately understand why. Blinded by tears and wracked by choking coughs, I was brought to my knees.

Given that the Arctic is often a very windy place, rendering pepper spray useless, Len and I have also brought along a 12-gauge shotgun loaded with slugs, the court of the last resort, so to speak—a windy day hiking and our suddenly surprising a grizzly who charges, or the stuff of lurid nightmares, a grizzly tearing into the tent as we sleep, the pepper spray perhaps immobilizing both of us and not the bear.

It may have been the possibility of this latter event that prompted Len to ask me which personal telephone numbers I wanted him to program into his GlobalStar satellite phone. He was sitting across the aisle from me on the flight up from Calgary, poring over the satphone's thick manual.

"Why bother?" I said. My mother, sister, girlfriend, or other close friends weren't going to be able to help in case of an emergency.

"I don't mean help," he replied. "I mean you might want to say some last words to them."

"You've read too many Everest books. This is a moderate river, and we're going to portage the big rapids."

"What about the bears?"

"Every bear I've seen in the Arctic, and who's seen me, has run away. And if they don't, that's why we have the pepper spray and the shotgun."

"I'm not going to use the shotgun," he said. "I'd probably hit you. If there's a bear in the tent, I'm going to lie flat and you fire over me."

This left me uneasy. "What if the bear decides to eat me?" I asked.

"I'm tastier," said Len, who is a bit heavier than I, and he went back to programming his phone.

Under the improvised mosquito tent, we cook dinner. On my last Arctic river trip, far to the east of here in the central barrenlands of Nunavut, we brought along a nine-foot-high, gazebo-like net tent, under which six of us ate in bug-free comfort. It wasn't my tent, though, and in the haste of our departure to the Horton, I hadn't bothered to acquire a new one, telling myself that we were going after the height of bug season and a few cold-numbed mosquitoes would hardly be a bother. This tactical error was made apparent in Inuvik, where the mosquitoes and blackflies were thick. Wisely, Len insisted that we get some sort of bug net. However, the only model we could find was about three and a half feet high, making it necessary to cook and eat in either a sitting or reclining position.

It's already close to midnight, and besides being sleepy, both of us are unhappy with the tight confines of the mosquito netting. Even though Corey's employer, the owner of the air taxi service, gave us a shoulder of caribou to supplement our larder, we agree that cooking it isn't our first order of business. We eat some soup and tortillas and retire to the tent.

It's then that I discover that Len is one of the world's great sleepers. Humming with two days of travel and the increased alertness that being in a really wild place brings, I'm unable to fall asleep immediately, and so I stare at the ceiling of the tent and the long shadows of the willow patterning its walls as the sun lowers to the north. Len isn't similarly distracted. His breath falls into a deep and steady rhythm, and he begins to snore, a snore the likes of which I have never heard. It's as if a two-stroke engine is backfiring in the tent. After coming all this way for some quiet, I'm stunned. Not for long.

I shake him and say, "Len, turn over, you're snoring."

He turns on his side and, unbelievably, goes right back to snoring, a vicious mean snore, a snore so loud I'm certain it can be heard in Inuvik, 300 miles away.

I shake him again. "Len, you're still snoring."

"Anne whacks me," he says groggily, "or goes to another room."

"There is no other room, Len." But he can't hear me—he's sleeping again and snoring thunderously, a look of great contentment on his face, as if he's left all his responsibilities behind. At this moment I realize that though I've done many day trips in the outdoors with Len I've never been on an overnight with him.

Resigned, I find my ear plugs—always useful in a storm when the tent is flapping—seat them firmly, pull the sleeping bag over my head, and try to fall asleep.

In the morning, quite chipper, Len says, "You look tired."

"You snored all night."

Abashed, he says, "I'll sleep in the mosquito tent."

"No worries," I reply, trying to make light of it—after all, no sense starting a long trip on a bad footing. "Let's have some breakfast and put together the canoe."

But before we can get the tea water going, we hear the unmistakable drone of a bush plane. Is Corey returning? For what possible reason? I don't think it's our pilot, for the engine sounds deeper than a 185, more like a Beaver.

A moment later, we spot the plane. Beaver it is, approaching from the south, not the west where Inuvik lies, and aiming directly for us. The pilot comes in without an exploratory pass to look for obstacles, taxis across the calm water, and eases the plane onto the beach.

Out step four anglers in chest waders, tan, stout, and with silver hair, followed by their guide, a young fellow in a British driving cap. They all wave and the guide gets them arranged on the stream before coming over and introducing himself—Craig Blackie, from a fishing lodge on Great Bear Lake, and also an ichthyology student in Ontario during the winter. The lodge is a forty-five-minute flight away, he explains, and this stream one of the great spots in the Northwest Territories for catching grayling. The four anglers are already hauling in fish and releasing them. Needless to say, after flying for two days to one of the more remote spots in North America, Len and I are astounded to be sharing our campsite with four men who look like movie producers. But not to grouse; they're out here, just like us.

We finish our breakfast and turn to assembling the canoe as Craig watches with interest. The canoe has a hypalon skin—the abrasion-resistant rubberlike material used in river rafts—and longitudinal aluminum poles and cross members that give the skin rigidity. All in all, the green canoe weighs forty-two pounds and has now run half a dozen rivers in the Arctic and the Rockies. As I watch it take shape beneath my hands, I feel as if I'm getting reacquainted with an old friend.

One of the anglers, who has temporarily given up fishing to watch the boat's fabrication, is clearly surprised by the seeming fragility of the craft. The ribs must be hammered gently into place over the longitudinal poles, then secured with baling wire, for in rapids the ribs will shift, and there's nothing worse than having your boat come apart around you, hundreds of miles from anywhere.

"Where are you going in that thing?" he asks with a French-Canadian accent.

"Down the Horton," Len tells him.

"Alone?" he asks in alarm. "Where's the rest of your group?"

"You're looking at it," I say.

"Have you no guide?"

"No."

Smoothly shaven, smelling of cologne, he shakes his head of silver hair, still troubled and not quite believing us.

We break camp and pack our gear in dry bags—waist-high containers made of the same hypalon as the canoe, with closures that fold several times upon themselves and seal with four snap buckles. Even submerged, these bags, known as "Bill's Bags" (named after their clever inventor, Bill Parks, the founder of Northwest River Supply), will keep your clothes and sleeping bag dry. The food containers have their own giant version of a Bill's Bag, known as a KOSS Bag (Kitchen and Other Strange Stuff). Everything has its place: the kitchen bag in the center of the canoe, Bill's Bags fore and aft of it, smaller waterproof stuff sacks in the bow and the stern for rain gear, cameras, binoculars, and bird guides—both Len and I are pretty avid birders. On the back of each of our PFDs (personal flotation devices, otherwise known as life preservers) is strapped a survival pack containing a compass, a space blanket (a flimsy reflective sheet that helps ward off hypothermia), some energy bars, waterproof matches, a whistle, and in Len's pack, the GlobalStar satphone, in its own form-fitting waterproof case. I have a vision of Len, after we capsize, floating down the rapids of the Horton and calling Anne, but I keep it to myself.

We don our PFDs; we put on our rubber boots; we trim the canoe, shifting bags here and there. When we're done, the boat looks very trig: square red kitchen bag amidships, snugged by oblong orange and blue Bill's Bags, the spare paddle laid alongside the gunwale, top grip toward the rear for the stern person to grab in a pinch, bungee cords holding all in place. The gear that was spread across a hundred yards of beach and tundra has been compacted to sleek bundles that now seem an intrinsic part of the canoe and give me the sense of being fishlike or birdlike—that is, having just enough scales or feathers to survive in this environment.

Only the caribou shoulder remains. A thoughtful gift from the air taxi service to be sure, but neither Len nor I is keen about taking it along. Even wrapped in one of our plastic garbage bags, it will perfume our gear, and we don't have the time to stay put and eat it, or dry it, the methods an earlier age would have used for dispatching this much meat during a hot week in August.

Craig and the pilot have been preparing a driftwood fire on the beach, circled by rocks and covered by a grill. They've laid out breaded lake trout fillets, caught yesterday at the lodge, and cans of vegetables as well as soda and juice, and invite us for what they call a "shore lunch." We decline, but their feast gives me an idea.

"Would you care for this nice caribou shoulder to add to your lunch?" I ask Craig.

"That's a lot of good meat. Are you sure?"

"You bet. Just let us cut off some for our dinner tonight."

Len holds the shoulder, I carve, and the French-Canadian helps us by slitting open two Ziploc bags with his fillet knife. Why he cuts open the plastic bags, with their perfect airtight closures, is beyond me, and beyond Len, who sends me a quizzical glance. The French-Canadian takes no notice. He places the meat I hand him in the cut-open bags and wraps it with great care, as if trying to show his appreciation for the gift of the caribou shoulder.

"I still don't believe you're going down the river alone," he tells us as he hands us the meat and we make for the canoe.

Len takes the bow, having diplomatically declined my offer of the stern, the steering position. It's my boat, he points out, and I should have the command seat on the first day. He'll take the stern tomorrow. Even though we're always polite to each other, today, with at least a fortnight of sharing cramped quarters ahead of us, we're being extra thoughtful.

I place the meat in the bottom of the canoe and push off with my left foot, letting it hang over the water, dripping, so as to keep the boat dry. Then I swing my hip boot over the gunwale, settle in my seat, and ask Len, "Which side?"

"Doesn't matter," he says.

Len's paddle is on the right side of the boat, so I say, "How 'bout the right?"

He strokes. I match his stroke on the left. And we're off, raising our paddles in farewell to Craig and the French-Canadian, who stand by their fire and wave.

The current carries us swiftly past the pilot and the three anglers downstream, all of whom are playing leaping grayling. An instant later, we're swept around a bend and out of sight. The country immediately becomes so empty it seems as if we're the first people on Earth.

Even after spending many years in the outdoors, in some very remote places, I always find this sudden change in consciousness a jolt. It's as if an unseen hand has literally flipped a switch in the universe. One moment I'm embedded in a world where motorized conveyances offer a quick escape to comfort and safety. The next, I'm free-floating in a world from which escape is extremely difficult—or was until the advent of global satellite phones.

The Arctic landscape hasn't changed since I first saw it two decades ago—shoreline sedges, dense willow, a moiré of green tundra, rippling and shimmering away toward hills dappled with the shadows of cumulus clouds—but I have to admit that the country's old edginess is gone. The mixture of genuine fear at being alone in the vastness of the high latitudes, and the lovely tension of facing that fear with no resources other than what we've brought along and the wit inspired by necessity, is diminished. The air taxi service's telephone number is programmed into Len's satphone and is no more than the push of a memory button away. The entire rescue services of North America would then be at our disposal, down to a huge, twin-rotor helicopter that can navigate through fog and find us by Global Positioning System coordinates. Len, leaving nothing to chance, has also accepted the offer of a handheld GPS from his law partner—a device that, with another push of a button, tells you your latitude and longitude, bouncing its signal from satellites circling overhead.

All this technology doesn't mean that we'll be less careful. Getting pinned in a rapid with your head underwater takes only a few seconds of inattention, and then all the satphones and GPSs in the world won't do you a bit of good. Nevertheless, the phone has given us a newfound cushion and is extinguishing an awareness that's always been part of these trips, what I like to think of as slipping through the world's harshness by a mixture of skill and divine grace.

4

ACCLIMATIZATION

Today the world is anything but harsh. The bugs fall behind; the sun shines; the wind blows gently, moving the shoreline willow like fur on some giant sleeping beast. Here and there fields of misnamed "cottongrass" sway. The plant is actually a sedge, topped by white pom-poms of plumed seeds that look and feel exactly like cotton. Below them, purple geraniums line the banks. The river itself is blue-green-chartreuse, top to bottom, and the sky and the earth seem limitless, a function not merely of the lack of trees but also of the shortness of the tundra's plants; 95 percent of their biomass lies below the surface.

The wind smells of greenery and faraway ice, and now and then it carries the clean scent of a fish leaping from the water. The banks speed by at a trot, small rapids play on the hull, an otter lifts its head and stares at us for a moment before making a chattering noise and diving out of sight. There is a plenitude of air through which we move without effort—no more than an occasional paddle stroke to keep us straight—and I suck in light and space in greedy lungfuls. I take off my bug jacket; I roll down my hip boots; I paddle in a T-shirt. It is open and free and splendid and beauteous, and I feel as if I've been paroled.

Len, who has brought along bug gloves, bug pants, and even bug socks—an entire uniform of green mesh, purchased quickly on the Internet and delivered by FedEx—gingerly unzips the hood of his bug jacket and lifts his nose to the wind. "This is magnificent," he says.

After a few miles, the current slows, the stream divides, and we must choose a channel, a choice that will be repeated hundreds of times in the coming weeks. One channel goes north, in the direction we want to head, but it has less water. The western channel carries most of the stream's flow. We go west and shortly find ourselves in a lake, with a range of hills ahead of us and the course of water dividing south and north around them.

We let the canoe float as I study the map, secure in its waterproof case clipped to the thwart in front of me. I take out my compass from my survival pack. The needle points thirty-eight degrees from true north, toward the magnetic pole, far to the east by Hudson Bay. I correct for this eastward declination on the compass's housing, orient the map, and hand it to Len without comment, not wanting to bias him with my opinion.

I open an energy bar, dip my water bottle into the lake, and drink it neat while Len studies the map—no need to purify the water up here. It contains no giardia, campylo-bacter, or nasty E. coli, all the little beasties that have made camping in the Lower 48 an exercise in disinfection. There's only fish and duck poop in the water and raven crap and the shit of a handful of mammals—bear, moose, caribou, wolf, otter, wolverine, musk ox, mink. Have I forgotten any? Beaver, muskrat, various mice. Oh, yes, and the occa-sional paddler. When there's this much water acting as a filter, that's not enough organic waste to worry about. In fact, the Northwest Territories are about half water, a result of the last Ice Age's melt off and the permafrost that lies just below the surface, preventing the lakes, ponds, and sloughs that have been left from draining away.

Len points north. I agree. We turn the canoe and paddle around an island of marshy ground, finding again two choices at the head of the lake. This time both choices go north. I stand, trying to gain perspective. The left channel looks dead and lifeless; the water in the right branch moves and drops.

We point the canoe in that direction and soon feel the boat's speed pick up as the current grabs it. Within another minute, we're shooting past small cliffs and through a band of spruce forest. A mile or so later, the stream slows and we have to paddle. After half an hour, without any warning, the steep riverbanks vanish and we enter a much wider body of moving water. We lay our paddles across the gunwales and stare at the river that will be our home for the next two weeks.

Upstream from this confluence, the channel is shallow and unrunnable—the true headwater of the river. Below us a wide channel runs between hills on the left and a great plain of tundra on the right.

"Sir," I say to Len, in my best imitation of Johnson to Boswell, "I give you the Horton."

"I'll take it," he says.

We have arrived. Sinking our paddles, we head toward the Arctic Ocean.

Mallards zip by, and young mergansers, still flightless, run on the water ahead of us. A V of swans comes upriver, wings beating in stately time. As one body, they gain altitude over us and descend when they've cleared the canoe, as if we were a mountain range they were smoothly traversing. The river bends and sweeps, bends and sweeps, sinuous turn upon long channel. A semipalmated plover hovers above us, calling in what appears to be a diversionary tactic to keep us away from its young. Named for its partially webbed toes, this species nests in the first week of June and its eggs take twenty-five days to incubate. Chicks can run after their parents almost immediately upon hatching, and twenty-one days later they're flying. I do the math: the plover's young should have been on their own well over a week ago. So what's going on? I watch the bird's pumping wings, black bill opening and closing, telling us something we cannot fathom. Such riddles in communication are among the more fascinating aspects of travel in wild country. Each day becomes an exercise in translation.

More small rapids come and go, cooling the air with their riffles. Round yellow rocks flash beneath the canoe, and in the deep pools—perhaps twenty feet deep—we can see the shadowy forms of large grayling, their caudal fins waving like the slowest of fans. The air is sweet, the water is sweet, the vast lay of tundra inviting, its purity magnified by the knowledge that its emptiness won't come to an abrupt halt. We're not in a 300,000-acre national park or a two-million-acre wilderness area, the boundary of which we'll soon reach. No bridge crosses the Horton, no ranger station sits upon its banks, no sign will tell us when we've reached a campsite. The nearest road is a fifteen-day walk to the west, if a person could walk twenty miles a day over this terrain. Millions of acres don't seem worth talking about up here. This is another planet.

We stay in the country's embrace throughout the long afternoon, stopping river-left on a gravel bar to have our own "shore lunch": seven-grain bagels slathered with tahini, sprinkled with Frank's Red Hot Sauce, and covered with Mezzetta roasted red peppers. We've left the latter packed in their original glass jars, and Len remarks that we could have saved weight by repacking the peppers in plastic containers. "Hey," I tell him, "we're in a canoe. Besides, we're on vacation." We also have a few pieces of elk jerky on the side (I dehydrated them the evening before we left), as well as half a brownie apiece, baked by my girlfriend.

Len, who has had only two girlfriends in his lifetime, both of whom he married, once again urges me to marry this rather attractive and competent woman, whom I've been seeing for two months, to stop dilly-dallying, to stop using birth control, and to get on with it. "She bakes great brownies," he adds.

I eat another brownie—they're very tasty—but in some tucked-away corner of my soul I would like to finish them quickly, fold up the aluminum foil in which they're packed, and have one less vestige of a relationship that has felt a shade not quite right, despite how much I like this woman. In fact, Len has heard me sing her praises. My reservations have been harder to articulate, at least to Len and other married friends. Can I tell them that in her presence I don't feel at home, despite my excitement about her? My concerns seem rarified, delicate, when compared to the texture of their lives: sick infants, sleep deprivation, balancing grueling schedules of work, exercise, and family time.

To my silence, Len says, "You're too picky."

"Perhaps," I concede.

That's all I can say right now. As I sit on the gravel bar, I feel an utter comfort, a tender regard for how this place surrounds me with its emptiness, and how my immense feeling for it seems without conditions, without pickiness. Not too long ago I had a similar regard for a woman, and I would like to know it again—that my world was made perfect by what others saw as her aloofness, her voids, her imperfections. Had she felt the same about me, I'm certain we'd be married. We'd probably be sharing this trip.

Len tells me, "You could wait forever."

"Maybe I will. I need to pee." I stand.

"So do I."

We walk up the bank, not wanting to pollute the river, though given the few people who pass this way it probably doesn't matter if we add some sterile urine to the Horton. But it's an untouched place, and we want to be fastidious; so many of our forefathers weren't. Gravel . . . sand . . . the vertical bank of loamy soil—climbing, we reach a different skyline. A flat plain of dwarf spruce, low blueberry plants, and tiny willow stretches off to a cloudless sky. Within a few seconds, mosquitoes buzz around our heads. As usual, I'm astonished at the survival strategy of these insects. As far as I can see, the country is devoid of any warm-blooded creatures except us. I used to think that mosquitoes wait day after summer day for the odd meal of moose, bear, caribou, wolf, or human blood, starving in the meantime.

But that's not the case. They feed on plant nectar; only the female must drink blood and that only before she can lay her eggs. Arctic species of mosquitoes like these can actually produce their eggs using the food reserves they accumulated while living in ponds as larvae. A drink of blood allows a female to lay a greater quantity of eggs, but even without it she can lay some of what are called "autogenous eggs" and ensure that she'll leave some offspring behind, a fact amply attested to by the billions of mosquitoes we've encountered. To be fair, mosquitoes are also pollinators of the northern bog orchid, a comely plant with greenish-yellow flowers, and so they contribute their little part to the beauty of the Arctic.

The life of the blackfly—a few of them still dive-bomb us—rivals that of the mosquito for adaptation to this environment. Like female mosquitoes, female blackflies need a drink of blood in order to develop eggs. They can, just like northern mosquitoes, store enough nutrients during their larval stage to produce a few eggs. But in some High Arctic species, the females take their adaptation one step further: they need no males at all to contribute sperm. Completely self-contained, they reproduce parthenogenetically.

Blackflies, like mosquitoes, also drink nectar and therefore may also pollinate plants as they fly between them. Nonetheless, I suspect their true evolutionary function, like that of the mosquito, is to weed out those of us who are psychologically and physically less well-adapted to the Arctic.

In this respect, both species have done a nearly perfect job, northern Canada having a population density of about one person for every twenty-three square miles.

Not dawdling over the view, we return to the river, followed by a few hardy bugs, whom the wind thankfully blows other places. We return the food to the lunch bag and snug it in its nook between the forward thwart and the bow seat. We've rigged the canoe carefully—it handles well with its present trim—but one touch remains. From the repair kit I take out some bicycle tape, the kind cyclists wrap around their handlebars. Soft and a little tacky, it's also ideal to put around the lower part of a paddle's shaft. Only several hours downriver, I've begun to feel the tell-tale signs of tendinitis in my wrists. The tape will help to relieve it by providing a more secure grip.

Len wraps his paddle as well, and the red-and-black tape, patterned like a chameleon's skin, adds another splash of color to our rig: green canoe, orange and blue dry bags, yellow and purple life preservers, T-shirts of white and heather, storm gear of emerald and gold. Like an exotic flower, we head downriver.

The sun slides west and north, the shadows lengthen. We look for camp, discarding one headland and gravel bar after another. Several hours go by. At last, a high, tree-lined bank, river-left, strikes our fancy. It's up in the breeze; the spruce provide some shelter; it has a couple of flat spots for the sleeping and kitchen tents. We're like prospective home buyers with no end of choices but limited time: after all, we do need to eat and sleep. We "buy" it, and begin the portage of gear from the canoe, across the boulder-strewn shore, up the steep riverbank etched with caribou tracks, and onto the bank itself, a full fifteen feet above the level of the river. In the spring, the water must roar through here.

Our personal dry bags are supplied with shoulder straps and waist belts for portaging, and we tote them on our backs, saving the kitchen bag for last. It has handles on both sides and we carry it between us, its ponderous weight hanging from our arms as we try to get through the boulders and up the bank without turning an ankle. Len scrabbles up the bank first and hauls as I push from below.

Gear at camp, we turn over the canoe, empty it of accumulated water—splashes and drips from the paddle—and carry it up the bank as well, tying it upside-down between two trees near camp. If it weren't securely fastened, a sudden wind could blow it away while we were sleeping, and if it happened to land in the river and was swept downstream, we'd be in a fine pickle indeed, though not in as dire straits as before. The trip would be over, and we'd have to wait a bit for help; but with Len's satphone, help would arrive in less than a day—weather permitting—not, as once upon a time, in weeks, when our failure to return would at last have been noticed.

We set up the sleeping and kitchen tents as a plague of blackflies swarms in the lee of the trees. I don my bug jacket and raise its hood. Len hasn't taken his off. We move food canisters under the bug net, light the stove, and cook a stir-fry of caribou meat, basmati rice, fresh onions, and dehydrated peas and carrots, spiced with garlic, ginger, and tamari, a lavish and sensuous meal here on the spare tundra.

Reclining on our sides like pashas, we eat from our plastic bowls and watch the blackflies crawl on the roof of the bug net. "Life's good," I say. Len makes a contented sigh. Then we do nothing, which is exactly what we've come for. We watch the bugs trying to get us; we watch the sun set and not set as it coasts along the northern horizon; we listen to the river making gurgling sounds. The sky contains one wispy line of pastel clouds, pink and orange, that soon disperse, leaving an immaculate dome, unmarred by bog or bug or boulder. It's easy to understand how the idea of heaven formed.

Len dozes. I go to the river and make a few casts with the fishing rod I brought along. Had I been set on catching a grayling, there were much better spots to have stopped and fished—small streams that entered the main channel, slow deep pools. Here, the river runs over a shallow bottom devoid of any hiding places or food. But I don't mind the lack of fish. I didn't come to fish. I came to paddle, to watch animals, to hike across the tundra, and to sleep what Ed Abbey, one of the most truthful nature writers around, called "the sleep of the just—the just plain tired."

And that's exactly what I am. After a dozen casts, I return to camp and find Len snoring. The sun has dipped behind a range of northern hills; the sky has grown dusky. The trees, the tent, the tundra seem painted in lilac. I ask Len to come to the big tent, and he says no, he's too comfortable.

"You're sleeping with the food," I tell him. "That's a bad idea."

He hands out the bear-proof food containers, the pots and pans, and I pile them away from camp, after scouring the cookware by the river and throwing the few food specks along the shore. With the pots settled on top of the kitchen bag, we'll have a built-in alarm if a grizzly visits.

I walk along the bank to my tent and crawl into the vestibule. Quickly, I unzip the bug net and toss in my sleeping gear as the blackflies whirl around my head. Diving through the small opening, I zipper the mesh behind me. Then I spend five minutes trapping and squashing the tenacious and unfortunate blackflies who greedily followed me. Little smears of blood blossom on the ceiling.

After loading the shotgun and laying it by my side, I place the pepper spray close at hand—no point in killing a bear who's just curious. I undress and throw my sleeping bag over me. Ever so faintly, from fifty yards off, I hear Len snoring. A moment later, the wind muddles the sound. With not a thought for blackflies, grizzly bears, or whatever is accumulating on my answering machine or e-mail queue, I fall asleep. And this too is exactly what I've come for: an empty mind.

The next thing I know, it's morning. Sunlight warms the tent, and a mumbling comes from where Len beds. I wonder if he's talking in his sleep. I can hear snatches about our plane flight, the river, Inuvik.

I dress, put on my bug jacket, go out and pee, Len's conversation still floating from the other side of the spruce trees. I walk over to the kitchen tent and find him inside it, propped on his elbow, a huge smile on his face, and his satphone to his ear. The phone's about twice the size of a normal cell phone, with a ten-inch-long antenna that aims straight to the sky.

"Lee," he mouths. He's talking to his eldest sister.

Going to our undisturbed kitchen gear, I take a pot and fill it with water at the river. A full one hundred yards from camp, I can still hear Len talking as if he were next to me. I'm amazed. Until Len's telephone call, I hadn't been able to measure the quiet. Now his voice gives the silence perspective, and I realize that without even thinking about it, he and I have lowered our voices.

When I get back to camp, Len is finishing his conversation. He powers off the phone and gives me a weather report from Jackson Hole (sunny and warm), tells me Anne wasn't home, so he called Lee, who will report to the whole family that we're alive and well, and would I like to make a call? He extends the phone under the lower edge of the bug net. For a moment I'm transported back to my child-hood—an older boy is offering me a cigarette.

"No, thanks," I say.

"She'd love to hear from you."

Len is a Quaker, but he could be Catholic. I do a quick reappraisal. The technology to stay in touch now exists, and he's using it: the good brother, the good husband, the good father. By comparison, my desire for solitude and detachment, even if only for two weeks, seems self-indul-gent, no, worse—irresponsible. The logic of the satphone is overwhelming and, to me, pernicious.

"Maybe when the trip's over," I tell him, feeling like a Luddite.

"Anytime you want," he says and puts the phone away.

The blackflies, numbed by the evening's cold, seem lackadaisical. I take off my bug jacket and cook four-grain cereal outside the bug tent.

We reverse the tasks of the evening before: we pack our sleeping gear in our dry bags; we put all the food con-tainers and cooking gear in the kitchen bag; we take down the tents and stow them on top of the food in the kitchen bag; we carry everything to the river's edge, the canoe last, and load each bag in the same place it occupied the previ-ous day.

There is harmony in this order, and a good deal of comfort, a sort of medieval universe. For the space of this trip, nothing will change in the nave of the canoe: the shotgun will always be on the left side of the boat, behind my seat; my water bottle will be by my right knee; the map case will be tethered to the thwart before me; my blue bag of rain gear, binoculars, and bird book behind me. The tents will always go up in the same way, and no upsetting news will intrude as we move downriver, or at least I hope none will. Perhaps, after reporting that we've arrived safely, Len will keep the satphone in his survival pack.

5

ROUTEFINDING

Unlike Len and me, Vilhjalmur Stefansson didn't own any detailed maps when he sledded through the Horton River country between 1910 and 1912. He had Franklin and Richardson's chart with Great Bear Lake to the south and the Arctic Ocean to the north, and he knew that the naturalist Roderick MacFarlane had supervised a Hudson's Bay Company post on the Anderson River to the west. The Anderson flowed to the Arctic Ocean, as did the Coppermine to the east. The broad outlines were filled in, but in between the two rivers lay terra incognita, fringed by the mouth of the Horton emptying into Franklin Bay.

Anyone with the slightest bit of topographic insight, which Stefansson had aplenty, would know that the Horton must head someplace in the highlands north of Great Bear Lake, and, like the other rivers nearby, flow to the Polar Sea. Consequently, Stefansson left Great Bear Lake, traveled northwest, and a few days later found, as he had expected, the valley of the Horton. This was hardly magic, as his Eskimo companions might believe, and something more than intuition. Like Franklin, Richardson, and a host of other Euro-American explorers before him, Stefansson had a geographic overview, a map in his head so to speak, one that encompassed not only this remote corner of the Arctic, but also the entire globe.

Stefansson found it interesting and surprising that his Eskimo companions didn't have such an overview. In their own country, they knew "every stick, every stone, and every creek-bed," a feat that seemed incredible to many white people. Stefansson, on the other hand, wasn't impressed. Such familiarity with terrain required "no other gift," he said, "than that by which the city dweller recognizes the street corners in the neighborhood of his home." In other words, years of living in a homeplace gives natives—whether native to the Arctic or to New York—an intimacy with their surroundings.

But take that Eskimo out of his home ground and he acted like a newborn. For example, one of Stefansson's companions, Natkusiak, whom Stefansson called "the best of all Eskimo hunters that I have known," went away from camp for two days, pursuing caribou. When he returned, he reported that he would have to go south for ten miles, then east the better part of a day to get to the cached meat.

It would then take him the entire next day to make it back to camp. Late on the day Natkusiak departed, Stefansson also went hunting, to the east, where he sat on a hill, glassing for caribou with his binoculars. Shortly, he was astonished to see a sled coming from the south. Who could be coming from those uninhabited barrenlands? It was none other than Natkusiak, following his trail of the previous day. In fact, the Eskimo hunter had made a great loop through the country and shot the caribou only four miles from their camp. Not realizing that camp was only about an hour from where he had killed the deer, he had followed his circuitous twenty-five-mile outward-bound route in order to return to his cache of meat, failing to visualize the shorter hypotenuse between the two points.

As Stefansson remarked, Natusiak didn't have an overview—a "map"—in his head; he was unable to navigate effectively in this new country. The explorer was quite clear that this bespoke no inferiority on the part of the native hunter. Rather, having a map in one's head, or knowing how to track caribou, depended on the sort of education one had received.

Within four weeks of leaving Great Bear Lake, Stefansson reached the sea, having at times abandoned the Horton's meanders to travel overland and catch its channel farther north. After resting two weeks at his base with his companion Dr. Anderson (no relation to the individual for whom the Anderson River was named), Stefansson returned up the Horton, hopping and skipping along the channel and across the intervening headlands. Slowed by deep snow, it took him thirty-three days to return.

Len and I, committed to the course of water, make speedier time. We have no dogs to feed; we don't have to run behind a sled—the river floats us along. Nor do we have to worry about finding the route, since if we follow the river long enough, we'll reach Franklin Bay.

We do, however, need to pay some attention to where we are each day. We have a date, two weeks in the future, when Corey will dip out of the sky and expect us to be at a precise location. I have a meeting on the day I return to Wyoming; Len has a court date soon thereafter—best not to be late. So in a kind of geographic suspension of disbelief—reveling in being out there while still being attached by a very long tether—I watch the map, a splendid blue, green, and white chart published by Canada's Surveys and Mapping Branch, at a scale of 1:250,000, updated using satellite imagery in 1983. Four of these maps will take us to the sea.

So far, we have come about three inches along the first map from Horton Lake, a distance of twenty-six river miles from where we began. Each day I keep track of the bends of the river and the headlands that flow by in slow procession, for if I don't, by the end of the day I won't have a very good notion of where we are. Len is not so compelled. With his GPS, he can pinpoint us on the map precisely at any given moment. But what if the GPS gets damp, goes haywire, can't function?

"That's why we have the satphone," he answers.

"What if it malfunctions?"

"Then we rely on you."

So I keep track of our position, primarily from my reluctance to put my fate totally in the hands of a machine that can break, and secondarily because I love the old skills of terrestrial and sidereal navigation. In fact, I am certain that without a map or compass I could walk back from the Horton to Inuvik, or even back to Wyoming for that matter, by simply looking at the sun and stars and remembering rivers and mountains from my previous trips—it's the map I keep in my head. Last night, just as a test, I penciled in our position on the map before allowing Len to tell me the coordinates from his GPS. I was within one second of the instrument's reading, a distance of thirty-four yards. Achieving such an accurate fix of our position after a long day on the river, going around dozens of bends and headlands, gave me great pleasure, like building a fine piece of furniture by hand.

I also like looking at the map for its innate beauty. I

watch it the way I watch my nieces and nephews, my increasing number of godchildren, and my dog—speechless at their young innocence. Nowhere in the 3,500 square miles represented by the map is there a house, a road, or any trace of civilization.

After a brief stint in the stern, Len has again taken the bow. He says doing the J-stroke—the steering stroke of the stern person, which requires turning the blade out and pushing laterally against the water so as to keep the canoe pointed ahead—hurts his forearm. Besides, he adds, there are too many decisions to be made in the stern. He didn't come here to make decisions—this channel, that channel; river-right, river-left. He wants to put his head down and just paddle, not captain.

This he now does, eyes half closed as far as I can tell from behind, sinking his paddle into the green-blue Horton and moving the river past the canoe, stroke after stroke. Subtly, unconsciously, we both increase the pace. Every ten or so minutes, I say, "Change," and without another word we switch sides, resume. The shore coasts by at a fast trot.

"We're moving," I remark.

"Yep," says Len, and keeps paddling.

This is to my liking. So many river trips these days, especially using rafts in the warm sunny weather that abounds in the Rockies, have turned into what are known as "float and bloats"—lots of food and beer, and little exercise. Likewise, as kayaking has become a sport of playing in big rapids instead of exploring rivers, boaters have gone to floating from play hole to play hole, not so much out of laziness, but because kayaks have evolved into short, blunt craft, turnable on a dime but unsuited for making any speed downstream in the slower sections of water. Having a companion who wants to put some effort into actually paddling, flexing shoulders, stomach, and thighs hour after hour, is exactly what I wanted out of this trip—the meditation of moving myself through country.

We take off our bug jackets; we take off our Capilene tops; we paddle on in T-shirts, passing a lone sick caribou, teetering along the banks, addled by flies. An immature bald eagle swoops from nowhere, passes over the boat, cocks his head down at us, and coasts on. A fat yellow-bellied marmot stares at us in astonishment from its perch on cliffs river-left. It gives us two warning whistles, waddles to the mouth of its den, its belly jiggling, and wags its tail, a happy-go-lucky soul. A mother red-breasted merganser—her head cinnamon and tufted, her body a paler brown—shepherds her dozen ducklings away from the surging canoe and into an eddy, except for one bold little guy who insists on scoping us out from ten yards off, ducking under the water and reappearing, his reptilian eyes beady, his already wicked beak carving the air. I wonder if he has survivor genes or those of the fool, if his behavior will let him thrive or result in his being taken out of the gene pool early.

Slowing his stroke, Lens asks, "Are you hungry?" We've been going at high speed for a couple of hours.

"I thought you'd never ask."

We find a gravel bar river-left, jutting like a fish hook into the river, and we park at its outer curve—in the breeze, away from the bugs. The sky is without clouds, the sun pours down. I take off my hip boots and trousers, put on shorts, and walk barefoot over the shoreline rocks. They're the size of lemons and oranges and feel wonderful on my skin—warm, smooth, hard. The beach.

Our lunch is the same—bagels, tahini, roasted red peppers, Frank's Hot Sauce, elk jerky, brownies—and just as good as yesterday's. When done, I walk to the shore, lie on the stones, and put my lips to the water and slurp. The river runs straight into my gut. Spread flat on the rocks, I see the water as a moving sheet, the sky a lighter blue above it, and I have a sense of swimming in the river as it swims within me. I cross my arms, put my head on them, and lie there, smelling the sun-warmed stones.

We paddle through the afternoon, the river looping through banks of low spruce and bare hills, the country stretching away larger and larger without mountain ranges, canyons, or forest to give any impression that one can't travel endlessly across it. Enveloped in silence, we paddle without a word. Indeed, it appears we'll paddle forever. By evening our muscles disabuse us of the notion. My shoulders ache; there's a sharp pain under my left scapula.

"Any thoughts to camp?" I say.

"I thought you'd never ask," Len replies.

We begin discussing various real estate parcels, and tonight our search isn't long. At a great bend of the river, we descend a small rapid and find that the rushing spring waters have deposited a remarkable gravel bar river-left: perfectly level, 300 yards long, bordered by sand dunes, free of bugs, and crossed at its lower end by caribou tracks. We bring in the canoe and ferry the gear up to the edge of the dunes; they'll act as a windbreak.

As Len cooks—pasta with tuna and a dill sauce tonight—I take a bath, first swimming, then soaping up with biodegradable soap on the gravelly beach, and finally rinsing off with a pot so the suds, biodegradable though they are, don't go directly into the river. I shave and shampoo my hair, niceties that I learned from my long-gone ex-wife, who was a great camper, backcountry skier, and rock climber, and who also believed that there was no reason not to stay clean in the outdoors. One time in Nepal, in late November, she bathed when the temperature stood at eight degrees Fahrenheit and ice lined the rocky stream below our camp. I was unwilling to join her, and a few minutes later, as she combed out her fair hair in the relative warmth of the tent, she said, "How much do you want to sleep with me?" I went to the freezing creek and bathed; and because I liked sleeping with her, keeping clean in the outdoors became a habit.

It's a good habit for the outdoor traveler to cultivate, whether accompanied by a bed partner or not. Like eating and sleeping well while camping, and staying dry and warm when the weather's foul, bathing reduces the differences between being "out there" and being back at what we call "home." With the playing field thus leveled, the common reasons cited for not appreciating the outdoors—I'm too dirty, smelly, itchy, tired, cold, and hungry—grow less compelling. Creature comforts attended to, one can then sit in one's own and the country's silence and ponder why noise has become such a necessary part of our lives.

I join Len, we eat some hot-and-sour soup as a first course, and I do the maps. Thirty-five miles today—no wonder our shoulders are sore. We finish dinner, we make a cup of tea, we recline in our Power Loungers—a sort of sling chair that makes sitting on the ground astonishingly comfortable. We watch the river sweep quickly around its big bend, coast by our gravel-bar camp, and shoot through another rapid that sounds its bass undertone from 200 yards downstream. We scouted this rapid before dinner, discussing how we needed to thread the slot between a boulder in the middle of the river and the left bank. If we go right, we'll wreck the canoe. But negotiating the rapid is tomorrow's problem. Now we sit, watching the river and the pale blue sky. The lack of anything to occupy our attention seems absolutely riveting.

We head to our sleeping bags when the light grows dimmer, maybe midnight, and sometime in the early morning I dream that I'm standing above a swimming hole the color of the Horton—yellow-green and perfectly clear. Two friends have dived in and failed to reappear. I grow concerned, then panicky. I dive in after them, but no matter how far down I go I can't find them. Desperate, I continue to descend; but I also want to live—my lungs are bursting. I kick toward the surface where I can see the sky, fractured above it. Breast-stroking, I head up, yet I'm unable to break the surface. It stays tantalizingly just beyond my reach. In another instant I'll have to breathe. I reach my hand to the sky—only water. It's the end; I'm going to drown. I wake myself before opening my mouth.

Groggy, and filled with the leftover terror of the dream, I look out of the tent. There is a dark cloud bank in the northwest, stretching completely across the sky, and the rapid downstream sounds ominous. Did I sense the low pressure and the oncoming storm in my sleep?

By the time we eat breakfast and pack the canoe, the cloud bank has covered the sun. The rapid looks much more threatening than it did last night, but still well within the capabilities of the canoe. With a few paddle strokes we position the canoe above the slot, then deftly shoot between the bank and the midstream boulder without mishap, paddling north in the cool gray light. I begin to shake off my dream of watery death just as we see another sick caribou, this one lying on the shore sand, its head hanging low, blackflies molesting it.

I wonder if, like the other lone 'bou we saw, it might be a victim of the warble fly, a furry little creature about half an inch long, with orange, yellow, and black stripes that give it the appearance of a bumblebee. The warble fly has no mouth—it doesn't need one. It lays its sticky eggs on the caribou's hair, and the larvae that develop, what any of us would instantly recognize as maggots, hatch and burrow into the caribou, tunneling their way like miners to the skin just under the animal's back. There, they cut breathing holes through the skin and continue to mature, getting all their sustenance from the caribou, who can be infested with several thousand of the parasites, each about half an inch long. Not only is the caribou weakened by the maggots, their many breathing holes can become infected and pus-filled. In the spring, if the caribou is still alive, the maggots squirm out of their breathing holes, fall to the earth, and become pupae, the inactive state from which new adults emerge to begin the cycle again. I have seen caribou buck, rear, and flee from warble flies like the end of the world was upon them. As well it might be. A bald eagle now circles overhead, inspecting the sickened caribou. Spreading its wings elegantly, the eagle perches on the top of a spruce tree and awaits the inevitable end.

The wind has shifted around to the north behind the oncoming front, and a steady cold headwind slows our progress. We put on our storm gear; we raise our hoods. Given the dying caribou, the patient eagle, the leaden sky, the unremitting wind, and my leftover dream, it's hard to feel as immortal as when we paddled through yesterday's sunshine. After only a short reconsideration of the warble fly's habits, however, I find mosquitoes and blackflies no hazard at all.

We make twenty-five miles against the wind—hoods up, paddling hard—and camp on another gravel bar river-left. It's not as inviting as the previous night's resting place. The beach rocks are bigger, and it's harder to find a completely level camping spot. Nor is the view as expansive—forest rises directly behind the shore. There is one consolation, however: not a single mosquito or blackfly can fly in the buffeting wind and approaching storm.

Len erects the mosquito tent with elaborate prepara-
tions, guying it in many directions to both rocks and stakes.
With inclement weather on the way, he's being more than
considerate of my sleep, and I tell him to join me in the
tent. No, no, he insists, he'll be fine with his bivy bag, a
waterproof cocoon that slips around his sleeping bag. Besides, he wants to test it out. Drizzle begins to fall, then
rain. I prevail on him—the storm seems like it's going to
be here for a while, why not be comfortable. After all, we're
on vacation.

He relents and brings his gear over to the big tent.
Even well guyed, it flaps through the night, but this too is
a consolation of sorts. It muffles Len's snores. In the low
gray part of the endless day, probably about 2:00 or 3:00
A.M., the rain begins in earnest, sheets of water pounding
the fly. The downpour wakes me, and I watch the roof a
moment, glad that I sealed its seams before leaving Wyoming. Then, dry, snug, and warm, I close my eyes.

In the morning we wake to hard rain, listen to it, and
go back to sleep after only a few words. There seems no
point in paddling in such ferocious weather. At about ten
o'clock, we cook in the vestibule, the stove warming the
tent to shirt-sleeve temperature. The purists of the bear-
security world would chastise us for not cooking out in
the storm. Wide awake, and with four cans of pepper spray,
we're not that worried.

After eating, we sit in our Power Loungers, sleeping bags around our feet, and drink tea, turning to our books, cozy as two British gentlemen explorers in the far reaches of the Empire. The image seems appropriate, for I'm reading James Morris's *Pax Britannica*, a history of the British Empire as it existed on the day Queen Victoria celebrated her Diamond Jubilee in 1897. Speaking of the noblemen and noblewomen who made up the British Raj, Morris notes that the poet Lord Byron met one Lady Wilmot Horton at a ball. I stop in astonishment. She was the wife of the same Wilmot Horton for whom the river outside our tent was named, and Byron, taken by her charms and the bespangled gown she wore, wrote:

> She walks in beauty, like the night
> Of cloudless climes and starry skies;
> And all that's best of dark and bright
> Meet in her aspect and her eyes;

It is a felicitous coincidence: Byron in Ceylon, Lady Horton in her gown, and I, almost 200 years later along the river that bears her name, finding out the background to one of my favorite poems.

We doze; we read. Len's Palm Pilot makes an odd distressed sound, and Len inhales sharply. For the next twenty minutes, he fiddles with the device, puts in new batteries, restarts it. He doesn't grow agitated; he says not a word. He works methodically, but his efforts are to no avail. Quietly, still without a word to me, he returns the Palm Pilot to the hard-shell waterproof case in which he also carries his GPS and video camera. Then he lies down and pulls his sleeping bag over him with a gesture that says it all: the Palm Pilot, containing six novels, his Rolodex, and his Day Timer, has died.

At about 2:00 P.M., the wind abates and the rain tapers off. As Len sleeps, I take the shotgun and walk up the hill behind camp, the forest dropping away after a few hundred yards to show a long broad ridge that goes on and on ahead of me toward the low and brooding sky. I climb, false summit after false summit, through some cliff bands, over ground that is firm and dry and lovely to cross. I stop, pick some blueberries, put handfuls in my mouth, and chew the sweet fruit, feeling ursine. I recite Byron's poem, and in no particular order follow it with the verses I have picked up in odd moments of being smitten with their music: Robert Browning's "Incident of the French Camp," Mathew Arnold's "To Marguerite," Hamlet's "to be or not to be" soliloquy, and T. S. Eliot's cat poem "Macavity." It is wonderful to hear the words pour into the sky, undiluted by any other sound, and to know that I will be surprised by no other hiker along the trail. I stand on a flat rock and pronounce Lewis Carol's "Jabberwocky" to audience of willow, blueberries, and distant dwarf spruce. Then I cock an ear and listen to them. They make not a sound, though an immense amount of activity is going on: photosynthesis; predation; decomposition; the carbon, phosphorous, nitrogen, oxygen, and hydrological cycles; all the complex biogeochemical activities that support life on Earth. Yet, not a sound. Billions, no, trillions of creatures living, reproducing, dying—and no noise.

By contrast, some of what we call "industry," "progress," and "economic well-being" back in the developed world is cacophonous: factories, jet planes, city and freeway traffic. Who would live in such din if they could have this quiet? Not many of us, I bet. Nevertheless, we've accepted the ongoing racket because we've made the assumption that it represents a higher quality of life. There is some truth to this—the Industrial Revolution has raised standards of living around the world, but the hidden truth is that noise represents friction, heat, wasted energy, in short, inefficiency. When we figure out how to reduce such waste, we may have less cause to take apart the natural world where silence and efficiency still reign.

I reach the summit an hour later and see undulating plateaus, exactly like the one I'm on, stretching to the horizon. The Horton runs sinuously from where we've come in the south, bends around the headland at whose foot we've camped, 1,500 feet beneath me, and loops to the north before disappearing into a grayish-green canyon. This corner of Earth seems vast, new, and empty. We're tiny in its immensity, but I have an uplifting feeling of self-containment: I look back the way we've come; I study the way ahead, 200 miles to the ocean.

The clouds from that direction stream very low, reducing the separation between earth and sky to a thin seam. I can actually stick my hand into the clouds, touching the moisture overhead. The gesture has little of the heroic about it. On the contrary, I feel compelled to kneel and smell the earth, moist and with the hint of ancient granite—we are on the very edge of the Precambrian Shield. I pick a few sprigs of reindeer lichen, stand, and toss them to the six directions—north, east, south, west, up, down—an old blessing a Tibetan showed me, which discounts no corner of the universe. Then I head toward the river, thinking of Lady Horton and all that was best of dark and bright meeting in her aspect and her eyes.

Back at the tent, I find that Len has also gone walking. When he returns we have afternoon tea, then dinner. The sun comes out in a swatch of blue between the clouds and the rolling hills. After a while, the clouds lower and we retire to the tent. I read on through the dusky light while Len studies his GPS with an air of indifference over his lost e-books. The day has been sublimely long, like one of those magical days from my summer childhood when life seemed limitless. It is a quality I would love to bring home with me: peace with focus, bountiful time, hurrying nowhere, leisure with purpose. I have made a similar resolution on so many of these trips, and have consistently failed to carry it through. Perhaps it is a resolution that can't be carried through, and so I return again and again.

6

POROSITY

L en is careful about his phone calls. He waits until I go for my morning constitutional—or for a riverside stop when I stroll off for a binocular sweep of the country-side—before dialing up. Nonetheless, I can hear him often. In fact, once, in a weird stretching of the normal bounds of sound transmission, I could hear him talking to one of his sisters from almost 300 yards down the beach. The morn-ing was moist with heavy clouds, the air thick, and I could listen to his conversation as if I were standing by his side.

He has set up a special voicemail account that only his law partner, Frank, and his family can use, and he checks it in case of a client or family emergency that would require him to fly out. He is most worried about his children—how they might miss him—and I can understand his con-cern: Madeline and Reed are sweet, and I love playing with them, holding them, putting my godson to sleep and smell-ing the vanilla-like odor of his hair. Fortunately, the river has many wide, deep, slow places where Corey could land his floatplane, and this sets Len's mind at ease. If need be, he will be able to get out quickly.

The satphoning puts us—or at least me, since Len hasn't really been out here before—in a very different relationship to this remote land. By contrast, I remember when I was fresh out of college and traveling in South America, exploring jungles and mountains, and checking my mail at intervals of a quarter of a year. In most of the places I was traveling, the nearest phone was days away, and then usually not working.

It was in the midst of this journey that my Uncle Michael, who taught me so much about the outdoors, died suddenly. By his side, I had first learned about quiet, sitting in the galley of our boat, anchored off the foggy New England coast, the periodic thump of waves sounding from the unseen shore. He would tell my cousins and me about faraway places where the water was crystal blue and the beaches blazing white and marlin as long as our cabin cruiser breached in the hot air. He was a marine engineer and traveled all over; from him I acquired some of my wanderlust.

Coming into Santiago, Chile, to check my mail, I walked into the American Embassy and found a string of telegrams and letters: the shocking news of his heart attack; the family's tremendous grief—he was only in his forties and left my aunt and my two young cousins behind; and the pleas to get home for the funeral, now all three months old.

It was a turning point in my life. I realized that one of the reasons no one in my family had ever taken any extended trips was the fear of not being home when such a tragedy struck. I had overcome that fear, as had my Uncle Michael (he died tending one of his ships in Japan). There was a cost, however, to freedom: I had missed one of the elemental passages of any family—bidding communal farewell to one of its departed members. Had it been worth it? There were 12,000 miles of country under my boots, and I had stored a year and a half of images, smells, and stories in my brain. Among our life choices, I had made mine, and I wasn't unhappy with it—struck dumb with grief at my uncle's death, yes, but still not regretful at being gone. In that era, there was simply no other way to become intimate with the outdoors, a family that called to me more than my own.

Now there is. We can have it both ways: be gone and be attached. Len checks his voicemail—in my mind, often; in his mind, occasionally—and, thankfully, it's always empty of bad news. I point out that there are some days when Corey would be unable to fly in because of the low ceiling. Len responds that there is no ceiling on a goodbye. This is true. The haunting final messages from the inferno of the

World Trade Center and the doomed hijacked jets are proof positive that all of us may soon carry cell phones.

We pass many fledgling eagles, both bald and golden. For the most part, they sit in giant nests of sticks built on the cliffs directly above the river. A few try out their wings, soaring uncertainly, a gust of wind sending them jigging wildly before they regain their equilibrium. Even then, their manner of soaring is nothing like the few adults we see, rising in the thermals with sangfroid. The new fliers climb with speed and exuberance, their body language seeming to shout, "I'm flying! I'm flying!" The birds still on their nests cock their heads to the sky, shake their feathers, and huddle miserably as the blackflies assault them.

Our camp this evening is on a high bank, river-left, with a few scattered spruce and a dotting of ponds. A range of low mountains runs to the northwest, paralleling the river's course, before bending over the horizon and disappearing into a threadbare blue sky. There are hardly any flies, or so I think—Len has his mesh hood zipped up, covering his face, while I cook dinner bareheaded and barehanded. My capacity to ignore the mosquitoes and blackflies astonishes him; but I point out that he has the capacity to ignore situations that I consider stressful, like living in a more crowded part of the valley and having a very steady nine-to-five job, five days a week. He considers

my riposte as we sit on the dry, soft tundra, the stove between us, the soup steaming. I serve it up—tomato this
evening—followed by a Thai stir fry made with green curry,
the fresh onions we brought along, and dehydrated vegetables and rice. If it were up to Len, he'd eat nothing but
pasta, butter, and salt until he got home to Anne.

We eat; we watch the river and sky. It is pleasant in the
extreme: almost 70 degrees north latitude and sitting in
light shirts. We wash the dishes and pots; we stack the food
containers away from camp; as it begins to drizzle, we go
into the tent and read. Simple tasks.

It rains through the night and early morning. By about
midday the front has blown through and roiled gray clouds
remain. We lunch; we repair a small pinhole in the stern of
the canoe where we've been taking on water; and by early
afternoon we're off, paddling down a stretch of river broken by side canyons. The wind blows just hard enough
upstream to make conversation difficult, and it's just cold
enough to prompt one to pee often, a time-consuming
affair if one has to pull into shore each time the bladder
calls.

We've solved this problem neatly by converting one of
Len's extra water bottles into a pee bottle. Coincidentally
enough, it happens to be yellow, so there'll be no mixing it
up with the other wide-mouthed Nalgene bottles that hold
our drinking water. We've named it YPB (yellow pee bottle),
and from the stern of the canoe to the bow, and back again,

we hand it, standing with our knees braced against a thwart to use it. Finally, we have to go to shore and empty it. With a scale on its outside, so we can measure how much we've peed in milliliters or ounces—a nice scientific touch, we agree—the YPB has quickly become a very valued piece of equipment, along with my hip boots that allow me to get in and out of the boat along a deep shore (Len has knee-high boots and has to be more careful), and our new parkas in which we remain dry no matter how much it rains and how hard we paddle. They keep out the rain while allowing our sweat to pass through the garments and evaporate.

Unlike at home where—given an array of retail outlets, the Internet, and FedEx—gear is almost instantly replaceable, here on the Horton, as on any long remote trip, it's ours for the duration. If it works well, it's respected and cherished; if it works poorly, it's condemned without quarter. One can see how cultures that had far less than ours quickly made technological objects sacred, especially when such objects made life more comfortable or safe. Fire, the bow and arrow, even the animals themselves, providers of food and clothing, became holy.

Len and I will of course be gone from this spare country, and back to the land of overnight Patagonia orders, by the end of the month. In the meantime, though, we live in that older relationship between people and their artifacts: no canoe will appear if we stave in this one; a sleeping bag, burned while cooking in the tent, won't soon be replaced;

and if the YPB is lost overboard, a substitute can only be found from our other water bottles, which already have their appointed use. It's a situation that breeds care, and that mindfulness is also something I try to bring home with me from these trips.

As we come down a long, straight run of channel, I see some brown dots on a hillside, river-right. The dots appear fuzzy, no sharp edges, and the pattern recognition is instantaneous. Still, I pick up binoculars and check before raising Len's hopes. I'm not mistaken.

"Look right, at about two o'clock," I say to him, not mentioning what I've seen so that his brain can assimilate the pattern on its own with no words to influence the newly forming image.

He juts out his chin and stares hard.

"Musk ox?" he asks, his voice rising in excitement.

There are five of them, lying on a knoll of short grass, noses to the wind, long black hair blowing sensuously around them. Their golden horns sweep by their cheeks, then curve up and out. Their eyes are closed; they look peaceful and at home.

We pull into shore slightly downstream of them and watch. Beneath the five bulls is a shallow drainage full of willow, and out of it another dozen musk ox begin to wander, cows and calves, young bulls. They have seen us, and, casting curious glances toward the river, they fan out over the hillside. The five large bulls get to their feet, also inspect us, and begin to graze. A few of the young bulls chase each other, butt heads. Their long, fine curtains of hair, reaching almost to their hooves, sway in the breeze, giving them the appearance of a monastic order. The analogy isn't far off the mark. They are Earth's hardiest terrestrial mammal, living in one of its most demanding environments, grazing in treeless country that provides no shelter. In winter gales, at fifty degrees below zero, they simply turn their backs to the storm.

One of the largest bulls walks down into the drainage and approaches us. He regards us curiously—I wonder if he's seen people before—then, with an air of dignity, he shepherds the entire herd up the ridge, over its top, and down into a hanging valley that is out of our sight. We have watched them for almost an hour and have grown cold, tropical beings that we are. We launch the canoe and paddle vigorously as the wind picks up.

We get no more than around the next bend, however, when a dark motion, among the spruce trees river-left, catches my eye. My heart trips, but I keep silent. A few moments later, I catch a full view: chocolate body, black legs, a honey-colored head and face, the unmistakable hump. It appears that Len hasn't seen it.

"Ten o'clock," I say.

He searches.

"On the bench. Moving between the trees."

He finds the animal in his binoculars and his body

tenses, then relaxes, and he takes a deep, satisfied breath.

"A grizzly," he says in wonder.

The bear is strolling downstream, browsing here and there. In a long stretch of open bench, he stops and eats blueberries with great concentration. Swinging his head back and forth, he sucks them off the branches.

Directly beneath the bear runs a side channel, and we pull onto the gravel bar that flanks it, abreast of the grizzly and at most 200 yards from him. The wind blows downstream, between us and the bear, and the gravel bar is raised in its middle. The bear can't smell us, and we're partially screened from his sight.

The grizzly, certainly one of the largest bears I've seen in the barrenlands of the Arctic, perhaps 600 pounds, gives no thought to what might be around him. He continues to munch with focus, stripping a plant, and moving on to its neighbor. Through the binoculars, I can see his tongue lapping out and in, immune to the stinging of the prickly bushes. His belly hangs low—obviously, it's been a good food year for him. Nevertheless, he's evolved to lay on fat for his long upcoming sleep. If the contented look on his face can be trusted, I'd say he's enjoying the process.

For a moment, I take my eyes from the bear and gaze up and down the wind-ruffled river to the sprawl of tundra and open valleys climbing to the low and overcast sky. Looking upstream, I can see the ridge on which the musk ox grazed. At this moment, I know as clearly as I ever will that the goal of this trip isn't the ocean. In fact, I've arrived. The enormity of the landscape is unimpeachable, the animals stately; both give a sense of eternity. A door opens and I step through, understanding that those of us who are currently alive may be the first people to view constant change as an endeavor worth pursuing.

The wind blows harder. We put on mittens and balaclavas, and raise the hoods of our storm jackets. The grizzly, in his thick coat, remains unfazed. He ambles downstream; we float along, matching his progress. He is too hard to leave.

The shoreline channel narrows and merges with the main river, and the current carries us toward the bank. A minute later, we approach within eighty yards of the bear. He doesn't look toward the river where we sit in the canoe, nor does he glance around, as do caribou, musk ox, or Dall sheep—all the animals who occasionally get eaten by predators. At the top of the food chain, he is splendid in his self-possession. We glide by. The last I see of him, he has his head deep in the blueberry bushes.

We have been immobile for over two hours, and the cold has crept into our muscles. When we're out of earshot, we open our thermoses and drink afternoon tea, though by the light in the sky it's already well on to evening. Warmed slightly, we recount our individual takes on the bear, naming his features and what he was doing, and comparing notes on how close he was at his closest point. It is curious: today we have seen eagles, caribou, mergansers and mallards, marmots and musk ox, but it is the bear who has fired our imaginations and made us more alert. As we begin to paddle and look for camp, we both agree that river-left, where the bear grazes downstream, is out of the question.

On river-right, perhaps two miles from where the bear feeds, we find a bench with a suitable campsite. The grizzly still seems close, but he's on the opposite side of the river. It's late, we're tired, and we call it a day. We carry our dunnage over the rocks onto the yielding carpet of tundra. Even so, the exercise doesn't warm us. We break out a considerable amount of warm clothing—shelled pants, pile jackets, fleecy hats with earflaps—and sit bundled, eating dinner and watching the opposite shore for the reappearance of the grizzly. He never shows.

Then the clouds to the north reveal a pearly edge. A few minutes later they're swept away, replaced by a rich blue sky and the golden ball of the sun hanging above the river. We shed layers, drink our tea, and watch the sun slide behind the far hills at midnight.

In the morning, the Horton is as quiet as a mill pond, and we're as slow as molasses. It takes us two and a half hours to cook, break camp, and load the canoe. Len, who has run some very difficult rivers in his kayak, mentions that our sloth would never be tolerated on a Grand Canyon trip where numerous parties vie to get away early each morning so as to reach the plum campsites by early afternoon. Needless to say, that isn't a problem here—we haven't seen a footprint, a candy wrapper, or any sign that a human being has traveled this way since Stefansson's sled trip ninety years ago. This, of course, is an illusion—not the absence of trash, but that we're the first to come this way since Stefansson. Corey's air taxi service, and two others in Inuvik, have dropped about twenty-five paddlers on the Horton this summer, a third of them in one large commercial group. Since anyone who comes this far to paddle is well schooled in the etiquette of wilderness camping, and a commercial operator has an incentive to keep the river spick-and-span, the place has remained unblemished.

We down our morning's dose of Vitamin I—four 200 mg tablets of ibuprofen—and set off. We have brought along a large bottle of the over-the-counter anti-inflammatory drug, the aging athlete's best friend. In short order, the sunshine, our exercise-induced endorphins, and the ibuprofen coursing in our bloodstreams make us quite cheery. We put our backs to it and the canoe surges ahead. A few miles downriver, still going briskly along, we enter a straightaway with a boulder field and high cliffs river-left. From the cliffs comes a plaintive cry.

Parking under the apron of talus, we scan with bin-oculars. I find the large gray raptor first, sitting high up in the boulder field, squawking. Len follows my directions and immediately says, "Gyrfalcon, I think." We dig out a field guide and see that Len is correct—a young gyrfalcon it is, about two feet long with corn-colored talons that match its yellow cere. It's a first field sighting for Len and he's thrilled, as am I. The farthest extent of the bird's win-ter range is the northern border of Wyoming, and I can count on one hand the number of gyrfalcons I've seen in my life. The bird makes a few more cries, peering up at the sky where its parents no doubt departed. Then it spots us and shifts uneasily from foot to foot, as if to say, "Oh, man, I screwed up big-time now. They told me to keep quiet." I ask Len if he doesn't think that's what the bird's body lan-guage is saying.

"You're being anthropomorphic," he tells me.

"I know, but it's a good story."

Unable to contain itself, the gyrfalcon cries out again and hops to a higher boulder.

"Let's back off," I suggest.

We return to the boat, and I use the opportunity to go upstream, away from the water, and answer a call of nature. Shortly, I can hear Len begin to talk, and when I return to the canoe I find him with a big grin on his face and the satphone against his ear.

"Roger Smith," he mouths.

Len has called our mutual friend back in Jackson Hole and is telling him of the gyrfalcon, whom we're still watching. Roger is a red-tailed hawk biologist, one of the first people to put miniature radio transmitters on the birds in Wyoming and track them to their winter grounds in Mexico. He was also the best man at Len's wedding, and Len and he were housemates at the University of Wyoming when Len was in law school and Roger was getting his master's degree in wildlife ecology.

Excitedly, Len recounts our musk ox and grizzly bear sightings to Roger, gives him an update on our weather, and extols the virtues of the canoe. Then he holds out the satphone to the air, trying to pick up the sounds of the squawking gyrfalcon—unsuccessfully. Roger can't hear the bird.

After a few more words, Len hands me the phone. I take it cautiously and say, "Hey, Roger."

"I can't believe I'm talking to you in the Arctic," he says. "You sound like you're just down the road."

Len is grinning hugely—the impresario of global communication—but I'm experiencing the same disturbing sense of unreality that I detect in Roger's voice, one that all innocents to new technology must have experienced, whether first mounting a horse, riding in a train, or speaking into a telephone. What is happening is beyond the bounds of our normal experience, although that's not a completely accurate portrayal of what's going on for Roger and me. Both of us are computer literate, use cell phones, and live in cyberspace during a good part of our working days. This is different, however. It's not so much that the satphone is technologically innovative; it's that it crosses some boundary that we have erected in our own minds as to what is appropriate behavior when one is "out there."

Roger seems flummoxed, and I'm laconic. He reminds me to look out for mammoth bones that could be exposed in the riverbanks we're passing. I say I will and to say hi to Margaret, his wife, and Kim, another mutual paddling friend. I give the phone back to Len, who signs off.

"Amazing," I comment.

Len smiles, a bit smugly I think: I have used the satphone; I have been brought into the fold.

We resume watching the gyrfalcon. The bird appears worried, casting glances over its shoulder at us. We mutually decide to stop harassing it and head downriver. On the right shore, a vast plain of tundra extends to a low plateau cleaved by several canyons. Overhead the sky has filled with gauzy haze, and behind us the gyrfalcon begins to cry out again. Everything is the same—the river bearing us along, rarely seen wildlife upon its the banks, the empty air like some restorative tonic—but everything is not the same. In this untouched place, I have a vague sense of pollution, which makes me feel silly, overreactive, and a bit precious. Nonetheless, the tainted feeling is there: I have strung a connection to the outside world.

On and off through the midday, I think about phones and trips and families. I think about how I'm selfish about my space, and the relationship I think I need to have with my surroundings, and how Len is not. This is probably one of the reasons he's a husband and a father and I still am not. Though, I counter, Roger is a father, and I could certainly feel his perplexity on the phone. I also recollect a story Len has told me concerning his and Roger's musings over the famous wildlife biologist Olaus Murie, who lived in Jackson Hole and whose work on caribou, elk, and wilderness preservation has informed so much of our lives outdoors. Len wondered if Murie, one of North America's finest interpreters of wildlife behavior from field observation alone, would have used all the modern gizmos—tranquilizer guns, radio telemetry, and DNA sampling. Roger answered, "He'd have been all over it."

The sky lowers. It begins to rain heavily. We paddle through the downpour and camp on a gravel bar. The river, charged with new water, surges along the bank, and we have to unload the canoe with care, lest it go off on its own. After we set up the tent, the rain tapers to a drizzle, and we decide to cook outside. A herring gull, water beaded

on its feathers, lands nearby and edges toward us. Closer
and closer it comes, until it's only ten feet off and eyeing us
expectantly. I wonder if it has gotten food from other paddlers and has become habituated to humans. It gets none
from us, and its patience deserts it. It flies off.

The rain picks up and sends us to the tent. In the morning, it continues to fall lightly, but the front hurries to the
south as we break camp, and we're soon paddling through
soft, cool light, changeable as the sea. For several hours,
faint blue bars shift among the swirling clouds, giving the
impression that clear sky must lie just ahead. At times the
incandescence shining through the overcast is fractal, a shape
in the clouds miming the shapes of the headlands, which
have their mirror images in the swirling eddies of the water. Vertigo is not the resulting sensation; osmotic passage
would be closer to what we experience, a passage between
congruent worlds of different scales. I start to feel less solid,
more so because of the precincts of strong odor we begin
to pass, saturating us more than rain: first blueberry, then
fish, a fruity scent as fresh and inviting as that of the berries
on the bank, but of a slightly different quality. Churned up
by the rapids, the smell of the char can only be described as
melons plus the sea. Canoeing through these olfactory curtains, I look down and see the creatures themselves: fish the
color of a mango's skin, green and pink, stacked in shifting
layers, noses all pointed upstream.

More avid anglers than we would pull over and catch

and release several dozen of these river dwellers, keep a few for dinner. Paddling feels too good to stop. We've eaten bagels fried in butter this morning, in addition to our cereal, and the extra fat burning in our bellies gives us strength. We keep up a quick rhythm—stroke, stroke, stroke—the miles unrolling beneath the canoe, the ocean pulling at us in a kind of reverse spawning run: we want to reach salt water as much as the char want to reach their natal streams.

As the midmorning clears and we float beneath a steep bank on river-left, I stand in the stern to scout the braided channels ahead. The wind is quartering behind us, the sky a sharp bracing blue, and as my head gains a few feet of altitude I smell caribou: musky hair, ruminated vegetation, a fermenting barnyard. The caribou, having congregated out of sight in a swale behind the riverbank, seem as clear to me as if they were standing within view: the dark patches around their eyes, their furry muzzles, their warm, tan coats. I can even hear the muted clacking of their ankle bones, a sound they make when on the march, though no sound is borne to me by the wind. Is this the play of my imagination or something else at work?

For a moment, I lose all track of where I'm heading. I'm caught in a world of smell that elicits sights, which in turn evoke sounds. I stick out my tongue and breathe in, tasting fish, deer, and sky.

I've known this sensation before, this stimulation of one sense causing the perception of another, and have spent some time investigating it. Technically, it's called synaesthesia, and everyone from the Chinese to the Persians to Aristotle has commented on it, the latter writing that there was a correspondence between colors, sounds, and flavors, violet being sour, for instance, and yellow being fatty. Sir Isaac Newton also explored the phenomenon, noting that the mathematical relationships among the seven colors of the visible light spectrum were similar to the relationships found in the musical scale, red equaling the tonic, orange the minor third, yellow the fourth, and so on. Sixty years after Newton's death, Erasmus Darwin, the grandfather of the more famous Charles, suggested that since the same laws governed the sensations of both color and sound, it wasn't unusual for music and painting to borrow metaphors from each other, musicians speaking "of the brilliancy of sounds, and the light and shade of a concerto; and Painters of the harmony of colours, and the tone of a picture. Thus it was not quite so absurd, as was imagined, when the blind man asked, if the colour scarlet was like the sound of a trumpet."

The saturated blue of the Horton sounds like the circumpolar stretch of the Arctic for me: empty yet rich, spare but comforting, quietly harmonious. I take a palmful of water in my hand. It tastes like silent sky.

Sometime between 1852 and 1856, Charles Baudelaire wrote a sonnet to describe these interminglings of natural phenomena. He called it "Correspondences," and critics ever since have heralded the poem as the inauguration of the French symbolist movement. However, Baudelaire wasn't so much an innovator as an observer of what thousands of people for thousands of years had noticed before him, and probably will notice into the future—if, that is, there are any wild places left on Earth where we can literally hear other voices, other "cultures" besides our own. He wrote:

> Nature is a temple in which living pillars
> Sometimes emit confused words;
> Man crosses it through forests of symbols
> That observe him with familiar glances.

What I haven't read about during my studies of synaesthesia is the sensation I'm now experiencing, standing in my canoe on the Horton River in the far northwest corner of Canada's Northwest Territories. I'm not merely transported to other places and seasons in an echoing interplay of my senses, what Marcel Proust wrote about in *The Remembrance of Things Past* when, after soaking a piece of cake in a spoonful of tea, he found the smell evocative of his Aunt Leonie, her old gray house, a town, the church, people, gardens. This is something a bit more than what Proust called "the immense edifice of memory," and goes beyond the sense of being watched by other beings, as Baudelaire and numerous Native Americans suggest happens when one is outdoors. I have the sensation of the world passing through me as if I were a screen. For an instant, I don't merely remember the smell, sight, and taste of caribou and char, I also feel *my* hooves in tundra, the river on *my* moving fins. I've transgressed my body, and through our joined eyes, I watch the world.

"Which channel?" Len asks.

I shake my head. The canoe is straying. We're a few strokes away from getting beached on an approaching gravel bar. I sink the paddle, pry it against the current, and point us toward the far right bank, where the water runs strong.

7

COMPANIONS

What goes on in Len's mind as we paddle along, I know only partially. In fact, I've glimpsed much less of his internal workings—longings, desires, hopes, fears—than I have of some of my other close male friends. He isn't a chatty guy, or rather, he is selectively forthcoming, one might say "politic," with the emphasis on tactful rather than shrewd. Of politics, the environment, the value of marriage, he can talk at great length. Of his own political plans or his own marriage, he is more circumspect. For example, we often bat around the various land-management issues of Jackson Hole, mentioning that if we only had some more ecologically astute politicians we might preserve the remaining open space in the valley. Yet, it is days downriver before he lets on that he's thinking of running for county commissioner. "I've actually thought," he says quietly, "that I could do some good in that office."

This news gives me great joy, and I announce my wholehearted support. He seems surprised. Is it modesty, I wonder? It certainly can't be that he suffers from low self-image—he ran the biggest conservation organization in the valley for years.

When I say he doesn't sound very excited, he responds that "Anne and I have talked a lot about what it would do to our family—endless meetings, less free time." Now I understand.

Of his life with Anne—trials, contentments, dreams—he says virtually nothing. I'm not put off by his reticence. Len raises a Victorian shield of modesty around hearth and home. Although once, when we're discussing a former girl-friend of mine (whom Len knew) and I confess that I'm not sure I could have dealt with her high maintenance, he says, "I've been dealing since the day I got married. Every married person does."

Paddle, paddle. Silence.

"What do you mean by that?" I prompt him.

In the middle of a paddle stroke he shrugs, turns, and smiles.

"Mergansers," he says, pointing with his paddle to the right bank. A mother and six ducklings eye us from a little cove.

Is he closing the subject or observing the immediate environment, as I, right now, am not? I wonder what Anne might say if she were in the bow of the boat instead of Len, or would she be just as private, joined with him in a respectful pact of silence about the inner workings of their marriage.

In a similar vein, Len says not a word about his first marriage. It's a buried subject. I never mention that I've remained in contact with his ex, that she remains the friend of many of our mutual friends, though I suspect he knows this. At one point, when we're speaking of what former relationships have taught us, he does allude to her, but not by name. "My first marriage taught me to work less and be more attentive," he divulges.

I suspect that if Len's first wife had wanted children they might still be together—Len's dedication to his work notwithstanding—for he is a family man to the core. After his first child, Madeline, was born, he'd wheel her by my house while out on his evening run, and pull her from the running stroller to show her off the way other men show off a new pickup truck. His delight with her was irrepressible, his enthusiasm for child-rearing contagious. Like his father—who remarried after Len's mother died, and began a second family—Len expresses his optimism best by bringing new life into the world.

On his father's birthday, Len calls to wish him well. We have parked on a gravel bar, and he shields the satphone under his storm parka's hood, for the rain is falling in sheets.

I take a photo of him: gray clouds and green tundra behind him, his eyebrows sprouting like tufts of wheat, his blue eyes gleaming with happiness as he talks to his father on the other side of the planet. I took the photo for Len, so he can remember this day in the Arctic when he called his father on his satphone. And I took it for myself, so I can remember my friend, still connected though far away.

When he's done, we shove off. As I change my paddle from one side of the boat to the other, I see that the black electrician's tape, which holds down the handlebar wrap on the paddle's shaft, has become slightly nicked and is coming undone. I smooth it down. Several rolls of the stuff were in the toolbox my father gave me before he died, and this roll, which I've brought to the Arctic, is the last. He would have enjoyed knowing that it was going down the Horton with me, since he lived vicariously through my trips, though he never hesitated to tell me how much he missed me while I was gone.

Once, long before the advent of satphones or even cell phones, I was sailing a kayak across a lagoon on the north coast of Alaska, three miles from the shore, when a storm kicked up. My friend Bill, whom my father knew well, and I almost capsized. We would have lasted about four minutes in the icy water, and I recalled in a flash—as the kayak heeled over and the sail caught in the waves—that it was my father's birthday, and it was going to be awful for him to have his son die on the same day. Then I dismissed my father from my mind. Grabbing our knives, Bill and I slashed off the sail, and the large double kayak righted. Shaken, we managed to paddle through a following sea, landed in the breaking surf, and survived.

Had we a satphone, and the worst had happened, I could have called my father and mother in my last numbing minutes, bobbing in the Arctic Ocean, and said what we all say at those times, "I love you. I'll miss you." Now, once again far away from my family, I think of my mother, still alive, and that she might appreciate a call from me. Maybe I'll ring her before the trip is done.

During the afternoon, Len continues to try to reach Anne, who has not been at home for several days. She has been horseback riding, hiking, doing things with their kids—or so he hears from his sisters whom he calls and who have seen her. Because Len keeps the satphone off between conversations, to conserve its batteries, Anne cannot call him. At camp, he tries once more to get her and, failing, calls his mother-in-law, where Anne often stays. This time he's successful, his mother-in-law, Beedee, answering.

"Have you been ravished by bears yet?" I hear her say.

Even woken from a sound sleep, she has her dry wit. She gets Anne, who is also sleepy and not nearly as chatty as Len. After all, the stars are out in Wyoming, not the sun, even though we're in the same time zone.

Len gives her a full report—weather, wildlife, boating conditions. He's lying on his side of the tent, I on mine, our piles of gear between our sleeping mats and the tent walls: duffels of clothing, water bottles, thermoses, pepper-spray canisters, books, the shotgun on my side. Our rain gear hangs in the vestibule; the YPB sits between our feet by the tent door. The person who tops it up must empty it. Socks and bandanas are clothespinned to a line overhead. The two paddlers at home in the Arctic, one talking to his wife, three thousand miles to the south.

Listening to Len, I wonder what Franklin would have said to his first dying wife had satphones existed: I wish I hadn't gone; we'll meet again in the next life; I shall miss you terribly? At least in the past, the mail gave us the luxury of a considered response or, as in the case of a dying person about whose sacrifice we might have some guilt, no response at all.

Finishing off, Len collapses the satphone's antenna and says, "They're all okay."

He sounds a little humbled. I thought I caught something from Anne that sounded like it was tough being a single parent, and thank god she has her mother.

He puts the phone in its waterproof case, pulls his sleeping bag over him, and in fewer than three minutes is asleep, snoring loudly.

I envy his powers of disconnection. If I had them perhaps I could have stayed home and been perfectly happy. I consider that proposition a moment and discard it. I listen to the dusky sky. I smell the willow, palpable through the mosquito netting. From upriver comes the sound of duck wings, the soft hiss of feathers in air. A drake mallard intones its low croak. Coming to the Arctic—for me, for Len—is just as much about connecting as leaving behind. I suspect that for Franklin it was much the same. As a schoolboy of ten, he convinced a friend to walk with him to the coast. Several hours later, Franklin stood by the sea, determined to be a sailor.

As we begin to paddle in the morning, Len tells me that if I want to call my girlfriend, to please avail myself of the satphone. He has made this offer at least half a dozen times.

"Thanks," I say, "I'll consider it."

"You ought to marry her, you know."

Does he want a companion in what he has called "dealing"? Would I not be an even closer friend to him and Anne if I were coupled, with children?

"I'm giving it time," I say defensively. "I'm trying it out." Surely Len can appreciate prudence. But when it comes to relationships, Len seems to know what he likes and dislikes immediately, and once committed, he's tenacious in the execution of his duties, marital or riverine.

He shuts up about my girlfriend and paddles unrelentingly through the morning, the best of bow men, two fast strokes to my one long one, hour after hour, even though I know he's in pain since he shakes out his hands when we change sides. It's a rare moment, though, that he'll ask for a change of sides. He leaves that up to me. Since I'm also in pain—we've been paddling eight to ten hours a day—I call for a change often.

We pass the Whaleman River, joining the Horton river-right. The main river is a turquoise green, the Whaleman bright blue, bigger than we suspected from the map, perhaps thirty yards wide at its mouth and running back through willow-lined banks into a broad range of hills. A moment after coasting by its mouth, I say, "Smell the fish."

I have my nose to the sky. Len raises his nose and says he can't smell anything. Two minutes later, my head is spinning with fish smell; it's as if we're part of the school. At that instant, just as we pass over a churning little rapid, Len says, "I think I smell them." In the tailwater beyond the rapid, char are stacked ten deep, like rose quartz flecking an emerald. We pass over them without a word; they in their world, we in ours, the meniscus of surface water between us. I wonder if our smell goes down the other way.

Just beyond this pool, the Horton makes a great bend to the south and heads away from the ocean for some seven miles before turning west and north again. As we curve around the apex of the bend, Len shouts and points to a brushy hillside river-right. I follow his paddle and see a grizzly bear bounding through the blueberries. Much smaller than the bear we saw a few days before, it stops, stares at us for a half-second, then runs, as if for its life, up and over the hill.

The river makes a few small zigzags, then straightens for several miles. At the end of this straightaway is the great canyon of the Horton and, according to trip reports from other paddlers, many rapids, some reputedly large. It's the end of the day, the river is already cutting down into the land, and small cliffs rise on each side of us. It seems foolish to go farther and have a poor campsite on some scratch of ground.

We pull in river-left and find a grand overlook of flat tundra and a few big spruce trees, under which we can cook. To the north we can see a limitless expanse of green plain dotted by lakes. Downstream, the Horton runs like an arrow toward the canyon.

It takes us an hour to get all the gear and the boat up the rocky little caribou trail that climbs the headland, set up our tent, tie down the boat, and arrange the kitchen.

Len has no more than soup before he tells me that he's beat and just wants to go to sleep. He heads to the tent, and I'm left alone on our high vantage point.

I walk uphill a ways and look back to the confluence of the Horton and the Whaleman. It's nice to be up in the air and have a prospect. Returning to the pod of trees and our kitchen, I make a stir-fry as two Canada geese fly overhead, honking sonorously. They make a short swing around camp to inspect me. Then a raven comes by, also inspecting me, followed by a herring gull, who hovers, swoops, and dives.

Sitting in my Power Lounger at the edge of the cliff, I eat my dinner and watch the gull wheel and soar and finally head downriver. A large bank of clouds has come from the Arctic Ocean, putting a thin haze over the sky. To the northwest, over the canyon, a sliver of yellowish light illuminates the horizon. No map has been made of the upcoming rapids, and this uncertainty is welcome. There could be big water where other paddlers found none, and the difficult drops they encountered may be completely gone at the present low water level. Anticipation vibrates through me. We're heading into a more demanding stretch of river.

I clean up and fetch water, lugging the two gallons several hundred feet up the headland—pleasant work, for it stretches the muscles made tight by paddling. Then I sit atop the cliffs, watch the river, and think that I haven't thought of the future for days: what I'd like to write when I get home; whether the noxious spotted knapweed, infiltrating my pasture, has been eradicated; and, other than Len's little fillips about my relational life, whether I will have a future with this new woman. Sitting quietly on a headland above the Horton, I visualize all these things as truly apart from me—figuratively and literally over the horizon. But I don't feel empty, which implies a container. I feel permeable, as if everything I brought along has been pumped out of me by paddling, and what remains is filmy, insubstantial. To achieve this state takes about a week in a quiet place with few disturbances. I sit a long time, watching the sun dip out of the haze and illuminate the landscape in a brilliant golden swath as it skids along the northern edge of the world before finally slipping into where I imagine the ice-covered ocean to be. Still, I don't move, watching the evening deepen into blue depths before going to the tent and falling asleep to the sound of rain.

It rains throughout the morning—hard, soft, silken, pounding. Len continues to sleep, as do I. We're tired and sore, and neither one of us feels like fighting the wind and the downpour. At last, we fix breakfast, and with tea in hand I sit in my Power Lounger and read. Len tidies up, sits in his

Power Lounger, and clears his throat. "Say," he begins, "you wouldn't happen to have an extra book I could borrow?"

After being lectured about the merits of the Palm Pilot, I am kind. Without a word, I hand over my stuff sack of novels and travel literature. It would only add insult to injury to mention the dead Pilot, for one of Len's other high-tech items has also turned belly-up, though from no fault of its own. We have unpacked, repacked, and unpacked every single container in our kits looking for the batteries that run Len's video camera, with which he was going to film our trip and show it to us each night. In fact, he pointed out how, given the right equipment, he could have downloaded video and e-mailed it to his family via the satphone so they could watch us paddling the Horton in almost real time. Mercifully, wiring our trip to this extent seemed a little much even for Len. He now suspects that in the haste of packing our gear on the dock at Inuvik, the batteries were also misplaced and forgotten. But the faithful satphone is up and running, and he does have an extra battery for it, so he feels at liberty to call home. After reading awhile, he rings Anne, and they have a livelier chat than the previous one, laughing and discussing whether Len should keep the beard he is growing and surprise their daughter by being "Mr. Fuzzy."

Sometime after midday, the clouds scud before the wind, opening great rents of blue, as if a whitecapped ocean had suddenly appeared in the heaven. The day turns increasingly fine, and Len and I—rested, hydrated, and well read—walk up the hill behind camp, where we see a young caribou. Holding our arms over our heads and bending low, we imitate two grazing animals while walking toward the deer. Startled, it turns and flees, but soon stops. It trots back toward us, peers at us, not certain as to what we are—the shape is familiar but not quite right. When we get within a hundred yards, it bolts and disappears over the next ridge.

We continue to stroll over firm ground, short dry tundra and plates of old stone, the plateaus and hills sprawling for a hundred miles in every direction. As we pass a small lake, Len decides to take a bath. He strips, jumps in, and emerges with gooseflesh. Since I have a scratchy throat, I decline. We return circuitously, through knee-high grass and willow, spying the tent far below us, a tiny fleck of blue, the only sign of civilization for as far as we can see.

Back at the camp, we eat dinner and attend to a necessary chore. Our bagels are gone, and we make chapatis for the next few days, mixing the flour and salt with water and rolling out the dough with a water bottle on the small cutting board we carry. The smell of the chapatis, lightly charring in the frying pan, is heady, and we slather the first one with butter and eat it on the spot. Then the second.

"I hope that doesn't dip into our stores too much," remarks Len, licking his fingers.

It doesn't. We have an extra bag of flour in our emergency rations, and a person can live pretty nicely on soup, chapatis, and tea while stormbound.

We clean up, repack the food in the bear-proof containers, and watch the sun set from the tent door, both of us delighting in the fact that we'll have fine weather to run the canyon.

Naturally, when we wake, it's pouring, the sky low and malevolent. A cold Arctic wind blows torrential sheets of rain, and the windward tent wall flattens and rebounds, even though it is guyed down tightly. The temptation to take another rest day is great. But if we linger, we'll never make the ocean. Besides, neither of us wants another day inside. Packing and putting on our storm gear in the vestibule, we break camp, load the canoe, and set off toward the canyon, the surface of the Horton leaping with raindrops. Below the top of the cliffs, the wind abates. A young gyrfalcon circles over us and calls, flies upriver, then returns to the canoe, hovering while emitting its high-pitched keen. Is it protecting territory, curious, or exulting over its having learned to fly? I wish I knew.

The river narrows, the cliffs on each side of us grow higher, the gyrfalcon falls behind. The wind drops, and the air remains cold. We paddle, hoods up, each in our warm, dry micro worlds of fleece and Gore-Tex. Len wears stretchy paddling gloves, I pogies—neoprene gauntlets that Velcro around the paddle.

The river slides into the canyon, into eroded towers and looming caves, into a phantasmagoric watery cavern of dripping red and gray walls. A peregrine falcon and a merlin swoop overhead. If we had been brought here blindfolded, I doubt we'd have any idea we were in the Arctic. We might be in Arizona, Utah, or New Mexico on a cold, dreary, autumn day.

The river, its volume constricted by the narrow canyon, swirls, sucks, and eddies, grabbing the canoe and releasing it suddenly. Gone are our rhythmic paddle strokes. We pull ourselves from clutching eddy lines, lean forward, lowering our center of gravity as the canoe surges and dances. Released, we float freely in the shimmering hiss of falling rain.

Above us, wavy veils of blue, like a daytime aurora borealis, begin to coruscate through the clouds. Over several bends of the river, perhaps an hour or two of paddling, they take over the ceiling, leaving a blue sky so washed-out it appears to be recovering from an illness. Around the next bend, the smoothly flowing river seems to stop in midair, creating a horizon line across the canyon. It's no illusion that the river seems to have fallen away: the Horton is pouring into its first big rapid. A few seconds later, we hear its roar.

We eddy-out river-left, pull the canoe's bow firmly onto the rocky beach, and walk downstream. Whitewater churns through a field of submerged boulders, creating holes as big as our canoe, places where the river, pouring over an obstruction, recirculates upon itself in a maelstrom of chaotic water. Run in a highly maneuverable kayak, the rapid would be a kick—the kayaker darting through the tongues of smooth water, zipping around the holes, and actually diving into a few to spin the boat around upstream and play. Of course, sealed into the cockpit of a kayak by a spray skirt, paddlers can right themselves using an Eskimo roll if they capsize. Indeed, in big water, the roll becomes no more than another paddle stroke, the kayaker moving in a 360-degree world, as much a water creature as a fish.

Our open canoe, loaded with 250 pounds of gear in addition to ourselves, is an entirely different animal, and we scout the route accordingly, pointing out to each other how we can slip along the left bank, the largest wave train just off our right gunwale. We then need to ferry into the center of the river, beneath the main force of the standing waves, to avoid a nasty hole. Twenty yards later, we'll have to move back left or else we'll smash the canoe directly into a large boulder. The route needs a bit of finesse, but looks quite doable.

We return to the canoe. Len pees. I head up to a bench of spruce and take a dump. Like nervous animals, both of us are preparing for escape or survival. From fifty feet above the river, the contours of the rapid flatten to a foaming white-and-blue spot in the river. Perhaps this is how all our travails look to an omniscient God—minor and diminished.

Back at riverside, the smashing waves resume their disconcerting proportions. We push out the canoe, I hold it steady as Len takes his seat in the bow, and I get in the stern. He puts his paddle on the right side. That's where it should be. To move the canoe river-right after the first wave train, he will need to draw while I do a C-stroke on the left side of the stern. Neither of us has said a word about this; it's obvious, and the other person's competence is comforting.

"Ready?" I ask.

"Let's do it."

Our hoods have been thrown back; the sky has deepened in color; we gain speed on the back of the river as I rudder us toward the left bank, just off the shore rocks that flash by, a gray blur. On our right, there is a wall of tossing water and white noise.

"Draw!" I shout. Len leans right. I lean left and bury the blade of my paddle in the Horton. The canoe turns as if it were on rails. We slide between the hole on our left bow and the breaking waves off our right gunwale, paddle strongly, and straighten the canoe.

"Cross draw!"

Len leans left across the boat, sinks his paddle into the river, and pulls hard. I pry outward without changing sides, shoving the stern of the canoe to the right while its bow goes left. The light green canoe arcs quickly back toward where we have come, and the giant boulder flies by our right gunwale. With a muted roar, the rapid falls behind us, and we float down the canyon in swift flat water.

"Nice," I say, resting my paddle over my knees.

Len turns around and grins.

Around the next bend of the river we find another rapid, then another, and yet another, six in all as the river rushes northwest. We stop and scout each one, discussing our route. We have no disagreements—we have both paddled a long time, and the safe passages seem self-evident. Once, when we have to enter standing waves higher than the canoe, we ship water, Len bearing the brunt of the crashing wall coming over the bow. In his storm jacket and pants, he stays dry. There's no question of going on after this section. We pull into shore, the canoe bloated and un-wieldy under our hands, and bail it out with oversize sponges, the kind people use to wash cars. The sponges can be compressed between the longitudinal ribs that lie along the bottom of the canoe, capturing water that would es-cape a bailing can.

We sponge out the canoe with few words, draining perhaps ten gallons of water, and continue to paddle. Not far downriver, we're swamped again. At our second bailing stop, we find human footprints on the sandy beach, a large-booted individual who has left a maze of tracks, more than likely a stretch or a pee stop; perhaps he had to bail. The prints are fresh, made within a day, certainly no more than two. With the paddler ahead of us, there's a chance we won't see each other.

The boat bailed, we move on. We soon reach a rapid that falls over a four-foot-high ledge. The ledge goes almost completely across the river, leaving a narrow passage river-right, too shallow to run with our loaded canoe. Uncoiling the painters from bow and stern, we line the boat along the shore, guide it over a two-foot drop, and bring it below the foaming hydraulic that could have trapped the canoe had we attempted to run the rapid.

The canyon is a bit wider here, forming an alluring pregnant shape—canyon, swell, canyon. Spruce line the tops of the cliffs, the sky is a vivid blue, the river glistens with slivers of light as it pours into the waterfall, sending up clouds of iridescent spray. It is hard to leave this place; it would make a lovely camp. Clearly, two weeks aren't enough to see this river.

For the next fourteen miles, we paddle through a broader valley, the water swift and riffly and undemanding. At a long peninsula of smooth basaltic rock, we stop and eat lunch, taking off our boots and damp socks to walk barefoot on the warm stone.

In the distance, we can see the river make a hard right turn and another stream enter from the left. It takes what feels like an hour to reach the confluence. A long rapid leads to it, and we run the whitewater without scouting, for it seems straightforward. Just as we make the right turn, avoiding the thrown-up, confused water where the two channels meet, the stern of the canoe slams into a rock neither Len nor I saw. I feel the jolt in the base of my skull, look down and left, and spot the sleeper—pale yellow, mottled green. It slides behind us. In the bow, Len felt almost nothing. The boat seems fine, though—no leaks, no broken ribs.

We paddle through quick water, in a steadily narrowing gorge. Ahead, the canyon curves to the left. On the right is a headland of black rock, carved smooth as an oyster shell. Shaped like an amphitheater, it echoes the roar of water. Just above this next rapid, a green canoe is pulled onto the left bank, with a hodgepodge of gear piled alongside it on the rocky beach. The canoe is a rental, the name of an Inuvik air taxi service written on its bow and stern.

We park nearby. It's obvious that the owners of the canoe are portaging, and we walk along the shore to see if the rapid warrants our carrying as well. A single tongue of river, smooth as oil, lies before us, flowing between boiling waves and holes. The bottom of the tongue is blocked by a flat, dark rock the size of a banquet table. Crashing whitewater lies to its left; directly to its right, the same. However, if we can dart the canoe river-right at the bottom of the oily tongue, there is a slim passage of standing waves, tall but not breaking, that will allow us to avoid the rock and its surrounding whitewater as well as the un-runnable rapid along the canyon wall.

Len and I stare at this crucial move for a long time—down, feint right, not too much, straighten, and escape—discussing our setup, and how we can't allow the canoe to build up too much speed in the tongue, for if we do we won't be able to make the right feint and will crash head-long into the rock. It all looks doable—not barely doable but very doable. It's within the limits of the canoe, and our skill, and it'll be a challenging run. After all, we did come to run as much of the river as possible. Neither of us wants to be influenced too much by the decision of the other paddlers, whom we spy coming back from their portage: a heavyset man and, much slower and far behind him, a heavyset woman, crossing several hundred yards of boul-ders. Both of them are in late middle age.

Len, ever convivial, approaches them, sticks out his hand, introduces himself, and introduces me. The noise of the river drones behind us; the man is soft-spoken and not forthcoming. He says no more than his last name, "Dunn."

He seems lugubrious and tired; so does his wife when she reaches us. They're dressed in old-timey clothing, like people out of the L. L. Bean catalog of two generations ago: dark wool pants, heavy wool shirts, leather boots that squelch moisture from their mid-soles. I can see the sole of the man's boot when he raises his foot up on a rock. He is the one who left the tracks upriver.

Mr. Dunn has a damp map tucked in his open shirt; his long underwear is fastened with buttons. He has a compass hanging around his neck on a red cord, and his ample cheeks are unshaven, his hair tousled. His wife looks beaten and exhausted, her face without color, her dark hair also awry. They both smell of wood smoke, and he tells us that they capsized in a rapid two days upstream and had to spend a day building a fire to dry their clothing and gear. Taking a swim has "frightened the missus considerably." He looks at the ground and adds, "This is a much harder river than I thought."

"We're really flat-water canoers," his wife offers, "and we were told that the river was flat mostly."

"When did you start?" I ask, wondering if they've been just a little bit ahead of us for days.

He tells us July 29—six days before we began. I can see Len hide his surprise. The couple is moving at a snail's pace, even if they've taken hiking days. They have one dry bag for all their gear. The rest is in backpacks and stuff sacks; their fishing rods are assembled and strung with line; a gallon can of white gasoline lies next to a lantern and one small waterproof ammo box. It must have been a mess when they tipped over.

"When did you start?" he asks me.

I tell him.

"You're moving right along," he observes.

"We only have two weeks," I say, apologizing for our speed.

"We have a month," the missus replies, leaving off what we hear in her voice—she hopes it's enough time.

"Are you portaging?" Mr. Dunn asks.

"I don't think so," Len says, and points out our route to them, describing the moves.

Mrs. Dunn takes an unsettled breath and says, "No, thank you."

"Good luck," Mr. Dunn adds.

We walk back to the boats together, where the Dunns eye our rig. There is not a single piece of loose gear in our boat—even the pee and water bottles are carabinered to a thwart—and anything that isn't impervious to water is stowed in dry bags. Len and I, in yellow and green Gore-Tex parkas and form-fitting PFDs, look like spacemen. Compared to the Dunns' beamy wood and fiberglass canoe, our hypalon craft seems gossamer.

A more graphic tableau of what has happened to outdoor adventuring over the last fifty years couldn't have been better arranged by a set designer. Much of the Dunns' gear is of "natural" origins—wood, cotton, wool, leather, and canvas—while virtually all of ours is made from petrochemicals—hypalon, Gore-Tex, fleece, pile. Had we capsized two days ago, only the clothes we wore would have gotten wet, and they would have dried from our body heat within a few hours.

Yet, northwest of us, on both the Canadian and U.S. shores of the Arctic Ocean, oil wells sprout, and a debate continues to rage over whether to drill in Alaska's Arctic National Wildlife Refuge. We're wearing that oil on our backs, the skin of our boat is made from it, and these petrochemicals have not only allowed us to fly to a remote place in two days, but also to travel through it in great comfort.

For those who love the wild, and watch it being taken apart by energy development, these are difficult conundrums through which to live. The Dunns aren't guiltless, though. Sheep and cattle still graze North America's public lands to dirt, fouling streams and displacing wildlife, and cotton is the most pesticide-reliant crop in the world, indirectly killing a pantheon of harmless insects and songbirds, many of them serving as natural pest controls.

One of the solutions I see to living within this ethical dilemma is to reduce our reliance on petrochemicals by developing hydrogen fuel cells. Then our existing oil fields could supply our needs for clothing and plastics, while fuel cells power our transportation system—quietly, it might be added. Organic cotton and more careful grazing of livestock could save a lot of wildlife habitat. These issues might have made for an interesting conversation between the

Dunns and Len and me—how each of us impacts the natural world while we're out there enjoying it—but the Dunns are in no mood for a chat. Mrs. Dunn is scared, and Mr. Dunn morose. Both are weary. They've gotten themselves in over their heads, and more difficult rapids lie ahead. Seeing two people who are having a jolly time on what, to them, has become the river from hell can only make matters worse.

The Dunns pick up their next load of gear, bid us goodbye, and start walking painfully over the rocks. We eat some energy bars, and Len says, "I wish we could do something for them."

I don't answer; Len doesn't expect an answer. The Dunns are in no emergency. We haven't come upon them capsized or thrown up on the shore, and offering to help them portage would seem a little patronizing, especially to Mr. Dunn. Going out there, after all, implies that you'd like to get through some difficult scrapes on your own. Mrs. Dunn might welcome some assistance, but then we'd be stepping into what has more than likely become a tiff over whose idea it was to run this river.

Feeling at a loss, we get into our canoe, shove off, and then any thoughts of the Dunns' welfare vanishes as we think of our own. We ferry upstream, eddy-out in the current, and I line us up. We sit the canoe, roaring white waves before us, split by the single, green tongue of water. We put in only a stroke or two to keep us pointed downstream.

A moment later, spray erupts around us as we slip over the edge, the table of rock, with its Scylla and Charybdis of breaking waves, looming off the bow. Even as I shout for his draw, in a move of utter perfection, Len leans right and sinks his paddle. Braced against the thwart, I hang my paddle far over the left gunwale and suck the stern toward it, the edge of the table rock and the crashing waves whisking by our port side. We straighten the heeled canoe and race downstream on the tail of the rapid, passing the Dunns, who sit on the shore watching us. We raise our paddles; they wave back, looking as sad as two people can be.

The river turns right, the canyon narrows, and we can hear the roar of the next rapid from a long way off. Its loudness intimidates us, and we park far above it, walking along the right bank to scout the holes and standing waves, all negotiable with care. Then we come to a house-size boulder, literally as big as a one-story cottage, sitting on the right side of the river. A trickle of channel goes between it and the right bank, but not enough water to line the canoe. To the left of the boulder lie fast-moving water and a rock the size of a kid's giant playball, slightly right of midstream. It appears we can run the slot between the house-size rock and the smaller one, avoiding the water farther left in the middle of the channel, where large breaking waves will swamp our canoe.

We continue along the bank, climbing a ledge that runs along the cliff face and affords a view down the canyon. After the theoretically runnable slot between the two rocks, a long, deep pool stretches from one canyon wall to the other. On the right side, cliffs plunge into its depths; river-left, a small gravel bar. Here is the spot we must land, for below the gravel bar the river narrows and plunges through a chute. To the right of the chute is a broad shelf of rock, to the left a craggy tower. In high water, the river also goes to the left of the tower, but now that channel is almost dry, with only a few pools of standing water remaining. The entire Horton, running through this one small defile, cascades into a frightening hole that sends up a rooster tail of spray. The waves bounce and charge at each other, flinging white spume into the air.

"Three-plus, maybe four," Len says calmly, alluding to the grade of the rapid on the international river-running scale. Class I is a flat river; Class II is like many of the rapids we've run. The last rapid that we ran and the Dunns portaged was a minor Class III. A Class IV rapid is a very difficult stretch of water with large confused waves and powerful holes. Only good kayakers—or canoeists in specially designed, decked-over canoes with flotation bags—attempt Class IV rapids.

This rapid will eat our loaded, open, erector-set canoe and spit it out in pieces. It is clearly not runnable in our craft, and if we are sucked down into the hole just beyond the chute, it is perhaps not survivable. The question isn't even about running this rapid, which is out of the question; it's our approach to the eddy-out point above it. If we mess up the first rapid leading to the pool and capsize, we might get to the gravel bar river-left, but our canoe and gear will be swept over the falls, into the hole, and perhaps be pinned and destroyed.

Standing on the ledge, in the warm sunshine, we discuss what we might do in terms of a portage to avoid the first rapid. The very safest alternative is to offload the canoe by the house-size boulder, carry the gear and canoe around its right side, repack everything, paddle down the pool, ferry to the gravel bar, offload the canoe again, and portage around the tower. However, Len and I are both paddlers—we have come to run the river as much as to see the surrounding countryside—and the technical challenges of negotiating the house-size boulder and the playball rock are appealing.

We walk back to the big boulder and find a way to climb it. Walking along its riverside edge, we peer down at the racing water beneath us and the playball rock almost blocking the passage. Len points out how the water does not go straight between the two, but has a caroming effect off the rock on which we stand. Therefore, if we do this run, he suggests that we paddle directly toward the house-size boulder, allowing the canoe to "pillow" off the rebounding water, into the slot between it and the playball rock, and on downstream.

I demur. I don't think his caroming effect is as great as he makes it out to be. I believe we should line up straight in the slot and run it directly down its middle, just at the edge of the caroming water. It's easier, I tell him, than he's imagining.

It's our first disagreement, and not over a minor point. The consequences of a miscalculation here are fairly significant. We are a long way from anything. The Dunns are not going to help us, nor is the satphone if we are swept into the next rapid, caught in the hole below it, and there's no one to throw us a line, and we drown.

We sit; we study the water. For several minutes we don't speak. I look away from the problem, trying to get some distance. Devoid of clouds, the soaring blue sky holds no counsel except that it's too beautiful a day to die. Golden light illuminates the cliffs, pocked with little caves and a few aeries of spruce. It is probably five in the afternoon, six, seven—who knows; I haven't looked at my watch in days. Turquoise and emerald, the river rushes downstream toward its white eruption beneath the tower. In the Lower 48, this stretch of river would be a national park or a designated wilderness area, commemorated on postcards and calendars. Here, it's just country.

I stand, walk back to the canoe, lie upon the shore rocks, and drink some of the Horton. It's always good to take what you fear inside you.

"What do you think?" asks Len, coming up to me.

I stand. "I think we should do it. I think we can do it."

"Thank you," he says, relieved that I haven't suggested the cumbersome portage. "But I think we should aim at the big rock."

I consider this. Len has been a Class V kayaker—in other words, the class above Class IV, very demanding boating—and has run a few rapids that I don't even entertain in my dreams. I don't want to dismiss his knowledge. Still, I know my canoe, have spent literally months in it, and I have the sense that it won't react like the thirty-five-pound kayak of Len's visualization. It won't lightly pillow off the carom of water. It'll plow through the pillow and hit the rock. I'm not absolutely certain of this eventuality, but I'm pretty certain. Still, I don't contradict him, for I feel that we've reached a personal crossroads, one that needs as much care to negotiate as the rapid before us.

During this trip, most of the decisions have been mine: initially deciding to go to the Horton, the logistics of getting here, what kind of food to bring, and on each and every day my suggestions about how to live well in the Arctic. This has seemed natural; I've made perhaps twenty trips to the north country. Now we're faced with one of those potentially dangerous outdoor situations in which the most experienced person should lead. Any adult who has tried to cross a busy street with several children can appreciate why this is so: negotiation doesn't work when hazards come quickly.

Yet every situation has its own logic. Those of us who have been married—and paddling a canoe is a form of marriage—make exceptions, fully realizing there may be unpleasant consequences arising from allowing the less experienced to take charge. Len knows much more than I about so many things: the law, finessing personal relations, and the needs of babies. I rarely travel in his world; he has quite willingly entered mine. In our balance of power, and more importantly because I love him as a friend, I feel it's time to relinquish some control despite the possibility of our taking a swim. In fact, it's because we may dump that it's important to give in.

"You've done a lot more difficult boating than I have," I say. "I'll go with it."

He nods, satisfied that I've taken his suggestion. We make certain everything is snugged tight—painters, dry bags, shotgun, bottles—and get in the boat. I feel myself take a breath, and I see Len take one as well. I look at the sky; I look at the cliffs; I'm pretty certain I'll still be looking at them in another five minutes, which is why I have consented to run this rapid in this way.

The first set of waves and holes goes by almost without my notice. My eyes are fixed on the rapidly approaching house-size boulder. We head directly toward it as planned, but it's coming way too fast; we're hurtling forward on a crest of green water and foam. Before I can yell it, Len shouts, "Backpaddle! Backpaddle! Backpaddle!" He is stroking madly, leaning upstream for all he's worth.

As hard as I can, I backpaddle with him. For one incredible instant, it appears we'll stop the canoe in midstream and be able to angle it left and down the slot. Then we hit the boulder head-on, not violently—our back-paddling prevented that—but hard enough to bounce the canoe crosswise, stern first into the main current. In a heartbeat, we're rushing sideways downstream, directly at the playball rock, on which we'll broach and be pinned, wrapping the boat in half and breaking it in two.

I spin in my seat, kneel in the bottom of the canoe, and yell at the top of my lungs, "Take the stern!" Simultaneously, I paddle two strokes forward with all my strength as Len spins, drops to his knees, and paddles from what has become the rear seat. The canoe kisses the boulder, slightly behind midships, rides up alongside it, and teeters on its right beam as the Horton comes under us and lifts. We paddle another stroke and pull around the boulder, the forward part of the canoe levered into the main channel by the enormous force of the river. We are now precisely where we didn't want to be. Waves higher than our head toss around us and swamp the canoe. Half full of water, we paddle through the haystacks, into the following pool, and manage to guide the ungainly boat onto the gravel bar.

"Well," I remark, stepping ashore, "that was exciting." I notice that I'm shaking a little.

"Is the boat all right?" Len asks, looking at the bow where it struck the rock. "I didn't think we'd hit," he adds.

"No worries. Your backpaddle saved us."

I'm not just telling him that. From the bow, he understood instantly the disaster that was about to happen, and he corrected for it.

"But you pulled us around the midstream rock," he says. "'Take the stern!' Great call."

"I could feel you paddling from behind me right away. You knew what to do."

We're talking fast, flooded with adrenaline, overjoyed to be in one piece, our estimation of each other confirmed—neither one of us clutched. We drink some water; we shake out our hands; we share some jerky and chapati. Fifteen minutes later, restored, we walk to the far end of the pool and stare at the rapid as it plunges between the tower and the shelf of rock. White spray shoots into the air.

Len suggests that we can paddle down the right side of the pool and land on the shelf that extends from the rapid to the canyon's right wall. There we can unload the boat and lower it three feet to the next pool, replace our gear, and continue paddling. It sounds reasonable, but we don't know what lies downriver.

"Let's look around the bend first," I suggest.

We climb behind the tower, through ankle-deep pools, along a broken ledge system, and find a tiny, flat beach of small, round stones where it is clear others have camped. We can see bigger rocks, still in the shape of a rectangle, where they guyed down a tent. The little alcove is snug as can be, nestled between the looming tower and a giant rock formation shaped like a schooner. We climb it and walk fifty yards along its top to stand on what might be termed its bowsprit. There we gaze downriver.

Just below the camp in the alcove, a rapid sweeps around the curve of the schooner rock. Over several hundred yards we follow our possible canoe route with our eyes—river-left, river-right, river-center—it appears runnable. Then we stop. A boulder blocks the only passage, and it looks very dicey to try to slip between it and the shore. The force of the river is too powerful, sweeping around the curve of the canyon, to let us approach the shore river-left with any degree of certainty. Below this rapid is another pool, the river surging through it and going beneath a small rocky headland, on the very end of which lies a barely submerged boulder that must be avoided at all costs. However, as in the case of the rapid below our feet, the river will quite possibly carry us into the canyon wall. It is clear that we need to portage, and a long portage it will be—three-quarters of a mile over broken rock on narrow ledges, up and down.

Len, fired with our success, or semi-success upriver, points out to me how we might just pull off this run without a portage. Talking hydraulics, backpaddles, and sideslips, he outlines his plan, gesturing with his hands. At home on the Snake River, with Highway 89 a hundred yards from its channel, running this rapid would be a challenging exercise of our canoeing skills, using a boat, it should be added, that was empty of baggage.

I hear Len out and then remind him that if we lose the canoe, it's a long walk downriver, preceded by a climb out of the canyon, before we'll find a place that Corey can land and rescue us. Of course, we could call for a helicopter and be plucked from the canyon immediately. Neither is something I want to be involved with—a satphone cry for help because we indulged our whitewater fantasies.

Len stares at the river. I follow the line he has laid out. It's just doable—if everything goes perfectly. But the canoe is not a kayak, we can't roll it, and we've been lucky once. I wonder if Len is remembering the short route description of the Horton we read while planning our trip. It cavalierly states that all the rapids can probably be run in an open canoe. Both of us had our hearts set on a clean sweep; our lining the canoe yesterday killed that dream, but perhaps we could have a two-hitter, given the rapid upstream around which we must carry. In higher water, maybe all the Horton's rapids can be run. Clearly, that isn't the case now.

"Let's portage," I say.

"I know," he answers with his elfish grin. "It was just a thought. I was testing you."

We retrace our steps and unload the canoe, tip it over, and empty it of water. Then, dry bag by dry bag, we portage our gear to the beach snuggled among the towers of stone. The kitchen bag is a brutish load—we slip and slide over the rocks as we carry it, having to put it down several times before reaching our campsite. Finally, we hoist the canoe on our shoulders and weave our way around the tower. By the time we're done, it must be close to 10:00 P.M. We'll do the second half of the portage in the morning.

We put up the tent and cook a big pot of minestrone soup. I mix up some hummus and lay it out with limes and crackers on the cutting board, set on a boulder that acts as a table. Very chichi. We lean against another rock and look upstream, but the rapids are obscured from sight by the tower. A few yards off, the Horton runs fast and green, the canyon full of its watery reverberation. The topmost pinnacles of the cliffs are painted with amber light, and in the remaining thermals an eagle soars back and forth between the canyon walls.

It is now surely close to midnight, and we started out in the early morning. There's not a breath of wind nor a single bug. We're at the very bottom of the river, as far out there as I think we'll get. We say not a word about this; we sit and take it in. Finally, we go to the tent and, with the voice of rapids in our ears, fall asleep. For once, Len seems too tired to snore.

8

DETOX

The rest of the portage takes most of the following day. Granted, we don't begin until some time around noon, hanging out in the tent, reading, and listening to the rain fall. That the afternoon and evening can be so fair, and the dawn so foul, remains perplexing. It's as if the Arctic Ocean has an almost endless supply of fronts to send our way. This hasn't been my experience in the past—the Augusts I've spent in these high latitudes have been consistently benign, even hot. Not today.

We begin to move as the rain turns to drizzle, but we're no more than halfway through the portage, lugging our dry bags along the slippery ledges, when the rain begins to fall in cascades. I think of Franklin and his description of portaging along the Mackenzie: "tedious and hazardous" with a false step proving "fatal."

I look down at the Horton, rushing twenty feet below the ledge on which we walk. One would not want to plunge in wearing hip boots and a forty-pound dry bag on his back. We use our paddles as walking staffs, and stumble along with the piggish kitchen bag. The ledge is far too narrow to walk side-by-side as we carry it, so Len goes first and I second, our shoulder sockets popping at the strain of holding the bag in front of and behind us.

During another trip we bring over our small blue dry bags, the shotgun, and the first-aid kit in its hard-shell waterproof container, toting them in our hands and hanging them from our life preservers with carabiners so we look like homeless people searching for shelter. Water runs down the cliff faces, rivulets stream along the ledge and pour into the Horton, and a curtain of water falls off the visor of my hood—it's as if I'm staring at the world from under my bathroom shower. We pile all the gear on a sliver of sand lining the rocky shore beyond the last rapid. Here we will launch our canoe. Only it remains—we've saved the most unwieldy load for last.

The wind has sprung up from downriver; the temperature has fallen; the rain feels as if it could shortly turn to snow. Len, having eaten a light breakfast, looks peaked, played out, and withdrawn.

I say, "How about some lunch before we move the canoe?"

We huddle in the rocks, turn our backs to the wind-driven rain, open the dry bag of lunch food, and eat jerky folded into chapatis, washed down with hot tea from our thermoses. We have to lean over our food, protecting it with our chests, or it'll be saturated instantly. The elk meat, bread, and tea bring my core back to life.

The color returns to Len's face, and he says, "Thank you for suggesting we eat. I needed that."

"Hey," I reply, "we're on vacation."

This rouses a smile from him.

We go back for the canoe, swing it over our heads, and walk the path, the ledge, the descent of the cliffs for the seventh time, resting twice on the way. When we get all the dry bags stowed in their appointed places in the canoe, our world looks right again: we're more aquatic than terrestrial creatures on this trip.

Len settles himself in the bow, I in the stern, and we look back to the cliffs we've portaged across and the magnificent tower, its top lost in cloud, the rapids breaking beneath it like tossing white tufts. It's not every day of one's life that it takes twenty-four hours to go less than a mile.

"I don't envy the Dunns," I say.

Len shakes his head, commiserating with what they are about to go through.

We push our paddles into the shore and shove off. For a long stretch the river runs with muscular power through the canyon walls. Buttress and couloir, headland and gulch, they march downstream alongside us. Young gyrfalcons weave over the canoe, calling to each other and trying out their wings. Herring gulls perch on the pinnacles like white gargoyles, cocking their heads at us before swooping toward the river and inspecting every inch of our rig. A brace of peregrine falcons strafes us, climbs, turns, and vanishes— Earth's first fighter jets. I wonder what these avian hunters are eating. I haven't seen a prey-sized bird in days, only predators.

We scout and run a fairly easy rapid, sweep around the next bend, and find a bigger drop split by an island. After appraising the route from shore, we choose the left channel, but what we planned as a straightforward run, well above a barely submerged boulder and hole, quickly turns into a serious catch-up paddle. The gradient of the drop is more than we calculated, and the current more powerful than we imagined. Its force carries us directly toward the thundering water. We paddle mightily, our stern clutched by the hydraulic and released.

One more long rapid faces us, 200 yards of big standing waves that we run along the left shore, the wave train higher than our shoulders. Around the next bend, the river slows and seems done with the canyon. The cliffs lie back and turn into hills. Congratulating ourselves, we drink tea and eat some energy bars before paddling around the next bend. A headwind stops us dead in the water, the river torn by whitecaps.

We begin to ferry back and forth across the channel, scurrying for shelter behind each headland. Spray flies over the canoe, drenching us. Heads bowed, we paddle, and when I look at the shore, it creeps by—no, sometimes we're blown backward. The wind whips at our anoraks, we take on water, and I think of Lear's plaint on the moor: "Blow, winds, and crack your cheeks. Rage, blow, You cataracts and hurricanoes." I say the words aloud for Len, and he laughs. At least we're dry, if not warm. Poor Lear was soaked to the skin and crazed with grief.

On we paddle—feet numb, hands stiff, shivering uncontrollably. I think of no more famous storm lines. Finally, we stop on the right bank and crouch among some large boulders that offer a bit of protection from the wind. We empty our thermoses and eat a second lunch. It has begun to rain again. I suddenly feel very thin. I've lost a bunch of weight even though we've been eating like lumberjacks.

On we go, hugging a point that seems to take most of the afternoon to round. On its far side, we find the Horton turned into a running sea of waves that comes directly at us. Paddling as hard as we can, we barely move along the shore. A bench of inviting tundra appears over the shoreline rocks. On it lies a copse of spruce, heeled over in the wind—shelter.

"What do you think of camp?" I call to Len.

"Soon as possible," he yells back.

"How 'bout here?"

We beach the boat and hobble up the rocks like crippled geriatrics, finding a welcome campsite on the moss and grass, in the lee of the spruce.

"Done," says Len, and we begin lugging the gear from the boat.

We erect the tent, one of us hanging onto it at all times, for it billows like an inflated parachute. We throw in our gear and tie down the boat. Back in the tent, we unroll our pads and sleeping bags. Len says, "I'll get water for dinner."

"I'll just close my eyes a minute," I tell him, "then help."

An hour or so later, judging by how the light has changed, I wake up, still alone in the tent. It's one of the sweetest sleeps I can remember.

We eat dinner in the vestibule—our concern for bears long gone, or rather, we're doing what seems appropriate in the situation. With bears spread thinly across the country, who would eat outside in the cold, wind, and rain after having been pounded by the elements for hours?

When I plot our position, I find that we've made only six miles today, bringing our total to 215. We are 158 river miles from the Arctic Ocean, and Corey is supposed to pick us up in three days. Even in perfect conditions, it seems doubtful that Len and I will make the sea. At about midnight, though, when the wind drops and the Horton turns glassy, we have a moment of reconsideration. We talk about setting off and paddling "through the night," which of course is not technically the case since it's still day. However, our bodies know it's night, and a few minutes after indulging our fantasy of "a heroic push to the ocean," we turn in and fall soundly asleep.

Even though we have given up this goal, we're still sixty-five miles from the other place where Corey would like to pick us up: the confluence of Coal Creek and the Horton. This is where Stefansson overwintered and where the channel, according to our pilot, is wide, deep, and slow, the valley broad, a perfect place to land the plane. Given the headwinds we've been experiencing, we might not even make this pickup, so we break camp early and find a gentle wind coming from behind us. It pushes the canoe along.

For an hour, the clouds give the appearance of lifting; we even spy an auspicious rainbow over the river ahead. But the clouds continue to hang low over the hilltops, and the tail wind increases. We scud along, seeing pods of caribou on the banks and swimming the river before us. The valley widens, and seams of lignite appear in the sandy banks that rise steeply for several hundred feet. Caribou tracks cross the precipitous faces, the animals who made them seemingly unfazed by the drops below. Whole hillsides of coal come into view, the beginning of the famous Smoking Hills. If coal weren't so abundant in the more accessible places of the world, there would certainly be tractors, barges, and mines lining these banks. Instead there are circular rocks—six to eight feet in diameter, three feet thick, and pale salmon in color—cleaved with geometric precision from the cliffs above. They lie along the beach at intervals of a few hundred yards, as if placed by a sculptor working with the idea of sparsity. Bald eagles appear from the clouds and soar by, ancient as the prehistoric birds in E. N. Kendall's lithograph.

When we stop to empty the pee bottle, I spy a pair of side-by-side grizzly tracks. One is almost as long as my boot; the second is as big as my palm. They are both perfectly incised in the fine gravel and touchingly human in their heel strike, arch, and five rounded toes: mother and child, heading for the berry patch. I put my fingers in the tracks, a way of closing the distance between us, and I'm suddenly very grateful that in all the years I've traveled in these places I've never had to shoot a bear, or even been threatened by one. I've been lucky; and I also indulge myself in the thought that I somewhat understand them.

We sink the third map, and when I put it away, I look back up the sprawling river, looping its way across the wide valley. The hills and plateaus—here and there a higher peak—recede back toward where we began, back into the clouds. Though most of the country is still unknown, it now has a line of intimacy through it: the course of our canoe, our camps, the animals, and the skies we saw. That view upriver, and the trail of vanishing bubbles behind our boat, is the picture I would take of myself, the way Len asked me to take a photo of him, leaving three rings in Horton Lake at the start of our journey.

At lunch I unfold the fourth and last map, and make our morning's float at twenty-three miles. Len, using the GPS, confirms our position. We've pulled into a gravel bar so long, wide, and flat that a small jet liner could land on it, much less a bush plane. It stretches up and down the river for more than a mile with no more than some hardy willow struggling to grow near its shore.

Rain begins to fall, and we put on our storm gear as the wind blows grit into our sandwiches, terminating any leisurely dining. We paddle; the rain stops; the sun shines. We put on and take off clothes, faithful to the weather's inconstancy. I don't find this a burden. It seems an enjoyable part of being out there—being comfortable no matter the conditions. I mention this to Len as we float along and have "high tea" in a sunny spell. I have rested my paddle across the gunwales, my thermos and cup on the flat part of its blade, along with an energy bar and some currants. I'm leaning back on a pillow made from my dry bags, my legs stretched out. I wear just a light fleece jacket and am perfectly relaxed. "All in all," I add, "I think I do better out here than back at home."

"That's because you're looking for the kind of perfection that doesn't exist in a person," Len answers, turning the conversation abruptly toward one of his favorite subjects—getting me married.

That was hardly what I was alluding to, but if he wants to go there, I'll follow. "No," I respond, "I only want to experience the same sense of being uplifted, of being in the midst of splendid country, of liking being there even though there's adversity. That's what I want in a marriage."

Len contemplates what I've said, and I add, "I wonder if some of the great marriages begin with less adversity, or perhaps more of a sense of being in a comfortable place with one's spouse than those marriages that require a lot of work." To illustrate my point, I name two marriages that I consider models of relational excellence, very old couples whom we both know, who live in Jackson Hole, and who by all appearances remain deeply in love after sixty years of being together. Without hesitation, Len agrees that these are people we could all emulate to our advantage. Then I name a younger couple with whom Len and I are acquainted. I mention how I admire the wife for how she's balanced partnership, motherhood, creative work, and a love of the outdoors. By my estimation, this woman reminds me of the very country we've just paddled through: strong-willed, beguiling, and needing some skill and care if you want to live with her.

Len gives me an over-the-shoulder deadpan look and a sharp lift of his bushy eyebrows, signifying that I'm out of my mind. He turns forward and resumes paddling.

Neither of us says anything; we don't have to. Our needs are different. In the marriage of this trip we've nonetheless managed to get along.

The rain begins as abruptly as it stopped. We put on our storm jackets, finish our tea, and paddle through a downpour all afternoon and into the evening, the wind slack, the rain falling in a steady deluge. Occasionally, I look down and see the rocks ten feet below the canoe, sliding silently by in their green and ochre world, mottled by the elongated shapes of grayling and char. When I look up, the world above seems just as liquid, the sodden shapes of caribou moving on the banks, the eagles flapping silently across the river, buoyant and drifting as fish.

We camp on a midstream gravel bar with a view up and down the river, steep emerald mountains rising into the clouds in both directions. We set up the tent in the steady rain, put dry bags, food containers, and stove in the vestibule, and disrobe in the cramped quarters. Quite astonishingly, our inner clothes are dry. This sort of comfort wasn't the case in Franklin's time, nor in Stefansson's, nor even in Len's and mine when we began to do these sorts of trips in wool clothing and ponchos. One similarity, though, I believe connects all four of us: our love of weather, space, and traveling through country empty of our fellow beings.

During the night, the wind blows so hard that my side of the tent—the one facing north, downriver, the distant ocean—hits my face, whips away, slaps me in the face again, and again. I turn over, put a pile jacket over my head, and go back to sleep. Everything seems of a piece now: the wind, the rain, Len's snoring, my aching shoulders, constantly sore yet quite functional. We gather no news except the features of the river. Perhaps the profound quiet, the numinous privacy, has affected Len. He has put away the satphone, and our world is the world solely within our view. I am filled with ebullience at this condition, especially because I know to what world I'm about to return: one spilling over with input. Not only have I managed to escape once again, but maybe this time I can really bring back the quiet for a longer period of time. Maybe if I imagine my office as a canoe—desk stripped to essentials, phone off, no checking of e-mail, at least not until the end of the day—I can hold onto this place. The resolution cheers me, as do the reclusive gray clouds, putting a lid on the earth with freezing rain.

In the morning, we pack quickly and soon face a headwind, strong but not creating whitecaps. We paddle through sibilant whispers—the river on the hull, the rain on the river, the wind through watery air. We say little, growing cold. Eager to be on our way and get to Coal Creek, we ate only a quick and modest breakfast and are now paying for it.

By midmorning we both crash. Famished, we stop when the rain does and gain some insulation by sitting on our life preservers. Shoving Fig Newtons, chapatis, and elk jerky in our mouths, and gulping tea sweetened with honey, we demolish an early lunch. With some calories warming my limbs, I climb a hill and take a distant photo of Len by the boat, he and the canoe in miniature but clearly silhouetted against the silver and gray river, flowing out of silver and gray clouds and dark mountains. He is dwarfed by the land-scape; he is absolutely noticeable. Of all the pictures I have made on this trip, it's my favorite.

We press on, the miles unfolding, the clouds lifting, the sun trying to break through. The skyscape is full of torn mist and rents of blue, all moving quickly from the Arctic Ocean, making the land seem bold and dynamic. A vast watershed opens to our left, the West River, and the Horton broadens with new water and grows murkier. It is now a mature river, not all that far from the sea.

To our right another valley opens—Coal Creek, de-scending steeply from a high plateau. The beach we coast by is sandy, cobbled with large, round rocks, and a small stream enters to our right through banks of willow. We beach the canoe just beyond the stream. This is the end, and it's anticlimactic. But there's no place left to go in the time we have.

We stand on the shore, shake hands, and give each other a hug. A large moose antler, green with moss, lies at our feet. It seems a sacred object, and we pick it up and fondle it. Len says that I should keep it, a memento of the river, but I return it to the sand. As I look at the antler, Len pulls out his satphone and calls his law partner, Frank, back in their office in Jackson Hole, telling him that we've arrived at Coal Creek and how useful the borrowed GPS has been. He removes it from its case and reads off the coordinates from the instrument: 69 degrees, 67 minutes north latitude, 126 degrees, 21 minutes west longitude. He tells Frank of the rain, the wind, the hard paddling, the rapids in the canyon, our portages. Then he asks for his secretary, Angie. When she gets on, he asks for an update on a client, hears of glitches in their computer system, and suggests whom she needs to call, and what needs to be fixed before his return. I walk down the beach and look north.

By river, it is ninety-seven miles to the Arctic Ocean. But by land in a straight line, it's only twenty-two miles. From here the Horton parallels the coast for another three-days' paddle, before losing itself in salt water. I can feel the Polar Sea in the air. But not this year, not for us.

When I come back to the canoe, Len is done with his phone calls and suggests that I call the air taxi service. Reluctantly, I agree. It really means the end of the trip. I get Willard Hagen, the owner and chief pilot, who says we'll be picked up tomorrow at about three or four in the afternoon. In years past—before satphones—one simply waited at the appointed spot for the pilot to arrive. If the weather was bad, or if the pilot had gotten behind in his pickups and drop-offs, one might wait a couple of days for his arrival. On several occasions I waited longer, and the uncertainty added to my sense of being out there. Now, it seems, we're truly calling a taxi.

The last of the clouds disperse, and the sun comes out in earnest. We strip off some layers and paddle back upstream, past the mouth of the creek, and make camp on the flattest part of the gravel bar, spreading our gear on the cobble to dry. Our pads, sleeping bags, tent, and fleece have grown damp over the last few days while we set up and broke camp in the rain. Within an hour, everything is as fluffy as if it had been put in a drier.

We place our kitchen down the beach and cook pasta in the luxury of sunshine and no wind, until our dinner is interrupted by a squall, and we have to dash to gather the gear before it becomes sodden. By the time we get everything squared away, the rain is gone, and we return to our dinner. Len takes a moment to call the owner of the company from whom he bought the satphone, telling her, with the excitement of the converted, that it is working perfectly at the very fringe of its service area, as she can hear.

After dinner, he calls Anne and talks to her at length, as well as to his daughter Madeline; he calls his sisters. His joy at having completed the trip and being close to getting home is clear but not contagious. When he holds the phone out to me, I decline.

"Too soon," I say.

The weather deteriorates through the night, and by

morning the ceiling is lower than the surrounding mountaintops. The wind churns the Horton into a three-foot chop. Soon it begins to rain. I call Inuvik and get Corey on the line. His conditions are just as poor for flying as ours are—he's fogbound. He says to call back around three.

We read, we sleep, we eat. When I call Corey in the late afternoon I can only report that it's still pouring and blowing, and he says he'll try to get us tomorrow morning—give him a call at 6:00 A.M. Our flight back to the States is at noon.

We read, we drink tea—it's like being on vacation from the vacation. Nowhere to paddle today, and nothing to interrupt the perfect and private storm weather, for it appears that Len has made all his calls. I think of Franklin in the early 1800s returning to Great Bear Lake for his second winter, and sending E. N. Kendall to Fort Norman on the Mackenzie River for supplies and mail. Kendall returned with warm clothing, newspapers, and letters, their news eight months old. In the early 1900s Stefansson, waiting in Point Barrow for his boat south, learned of the *Titanic*'s sinking from the whaler *Elvira*, three months and ten days after the great ocean liner foundered in the North Atlantic. Now, in the early 2000s, the time lag between the occurrence of a newsworthy event and one's hearing of it has shrunk to the thinnest of margins. In fact, even here on the Horton the blessing of uncluttered mental space is no longer a function of remoteness but of desire.

It rains into the early evening, and when it lets up, Len and I take walks in different directions—he down the beach, I up the creek—each of us then exploring where the other went. We don't find Stefansson's small log cabin. Perhaps it has collapsed and been covered over by willow. Not seeing it doesn't displease me. I prefer the picture that I have in my mind: the rough structure deep in the winter trees, surrounded by sleds and dogs and Eskimos in their caribou parkas.

After dinner Len is back on the phone, touching base with family and telling them of the delay because of the weather. When done, he suggests I call my girlfriend because she'll worry about me. We were supposed to be out today, and I certainly would have called her from Inuvik if that had been the case. In this light, it's hard to keep myself sequestered in the bubble of the trip. She knows Len has the satphone; she knows when I said I would call her from Inuvik. She will wonder, if we're stormbound, why I was so thoughtless, with a satphone at hand, not to call her.

I walk up the beach, dial her up, and talk for a few minutes. She could be next door, the connection is so clear, but there is still a disconnect far wider than, say, talking between Jackson and Jakarta. There each party is at least in the same world—house, appliances, roads, connected by CNN and BBC and NPR, the Net. Here, I feel permeated by a totally different world, one without acronyms, or words, for that matter. I'm having a hard time with the latter. I say, "I can smell the Arctic Ocean," and promise that I will call from a land line when we get to Inuvik.

Collapsing the antenna, I walk back toward camp and am surprised to see Len standing on the beach, his face tilted up to the sky, his arms open, palms spread, like an angel. He turns a slow stately circle as if embracing the mountains, the rivers, and the clouds. It is a gesture of such sublime thankfulness that I cannot intrude. I walk away, leaving him to his own good-byes.

In the morning our ceiling is higher, Inuvik's lower. Corey says to call in another two hours. We take apart the canoe, a task that reminds me of closing up a summer home. The frail little craft has completed another Arctic river, its hull and ribs seeming a little heavier with memories. We strike the tent and bring all the dry bags to the shore. Then we wait, dressed in our warmest clothing because the wind has picked up. The time passes, and the likelihood of our catching our jet flight diminishes.

I call Corey again. He's taken off, I'm told. Then I decide to call my mother, knowing that she keeps track of the day I'm supposed to return to civilization and that she'll worry if she doesn't hear from me, despite my reminders to her about bush planes not running on the same schedules as commercial airliners. Calling will also be a way of showing Len that I'm not a complete technophobe.

"You're where?" she shouts.

"The Horton River."

This connection, to the other side of North America, is sketchy.

"We're waiting for the bush plane to fly to Inuvik."

"Where's that?"

"Near the Arctic Ocean."

"Oh," she replies as if my geographic location is now crystal clear. "Just be careful, and call me when you get home."

I power off, relieved in a way. My mother, who has a great capacity to imagine disaster, still prefers silence from the field. Her son is safe only when he steps through his own door.

Within an hour, we hear the drone of the 185, coming from the northwest. A minute later, we see the insectlike spread of its wings. Corey passes overhead, banks, and lands downstream, into the wind. He taxis into shore, and we load everything into the back of the 185. Len and I swap the seats we occupied on the way out—he takes front right, next to Corey, I the rear. I'm the last one in, and before boarding, I turn to the beach and give a farewell nod to the river, our third companion.

It takes three tries for Corey to get airborne—the plane wants to head directly into the wind and the wall of mountains on the left side of the river. Corey fights the yoke, the engine roaring. Finally, he breaks the pontoons free. In flight, but not by much, we skim the water, gaining altitude slowly. Then the river sinks below us. To the north lies the slate-blue line of the Arctic Ocean. Corey turns west and flies through clouds and rain. We pass over lakes and ponds, other rivers and many canyons, plateaus of empty tundra, and no sign of people until we reach Inuvik two hours later. There we see our jet rushing down the runway and lifting into the sky before turning south.

"You missed it," says Corey.

At the dock, we make a hasty call to the airline. I have that meeting to attend, starting tomorrow evening, and Len, besides his upcoming court date, wants to get home to his family. We discover that another flight leaves in an hour, but it's completely booked and doesn't go directly to Calgary as ours did. It stops at Norman Wells, Yellowknife, and Edmonton.

"You can try going standby," says the attendant, "but you'd better get here right away."

Corey drives us to the airport, and while Len waits in line with our tickets, I empty all the dry bags, putting our gear and the canoe into the four giant airline duffels. The terminal, a single large room, is filled with natives in parkas and oil workers in coveralls, and not one of them gives me a second glance as I take apart the shotgun. I'm still wearing my hip boots, my fleece, and my Gore-Tex, and I start to smell myself in the heat.

Len joins me, standby tickets in hand, and we step out of our rubber boots and into trail shoes. He squeezes the red bags shut as I zip them. With the gear tossed in rather than neatly packed, it's a miracle we get the bags closed. Then we drag the lot to the counter, where we cool our heels.

This has all happened too fast. Three and a half hours ago we were sitting on the banks of the Horton River in the cold Arctic wind; now we're standing in line with dozens of people in a steamy building. Franklin took half a year to get home, Stefansson months. We are reconnecting in two days. Then again, our disconnect—home to the river—was equally fast.

Standby passenger after standby passenger is called and goes through the exit doors. The plane is fully loaded; no one is left. It appears all our rushing was for nothing. Then the counter attendant disappears into a back room, re-emerges, and calls our names. We drag the bags across her scales and into the hands of several burly men. We head out the exit doors—there's no security up here—and walk onto the tarmac. I feel light, disembodied. The wind and the river water still lingering on my face are like temporary shields holding off this bombardment of sights and sounds.

All afternoon we make our way south, getting off the plane in Norman Wells, Yellowknife, and Edmonton to walk around. Tobacco smoke, perfume, deep-fried food, floor polish—a new world, a familiar world, begins. The weather turns tropically warm.

Our luggage doesn't make it to Calgary. After checking in at our hotel, we take a taxi to the Indian restaurant where we enjoyed a dinner on the way up. The evening temperature is in the mid-seventies. Women in halter tops and cutoff jeans stride on the sidewalk, and the traffic moves by, headlights on, for it's now actually dark. Still unshowered and in our river clothes, we look and smell pretty ragged. For a moment I think of my ex-wife and wonder if she would have bathed in those freezing downpours. Len and I clink glasses of beer.

"Thank you for this trip, Leonard," I say.

"Thank *you*," he answers. "I wouldn't have gotten away otherwise."

The Indian waitress doesn't seem to mind our appearance—she has seen other travelers from the far north before—and we leave her a good tip.

At the hotel, our gear has arrived. We shower and get into bed. It has been a long day. In fact, it seems as if it has been one continuous day since we flew into Horton Lake. It never grew dark, after all.

I'm tired, very tired, but I can't sleep, and it isn't from nervous energy. The air conditioner throbs in the window, and I can hear the soda vending machine vibrating down the hall. On the night table between Len's and my bed, the electric clock hums. Surprising me, he breathes softly, peacefully—no snores at all. From the next room, TV laughter sounds and a phone rings. When they grow quiet, I can hear the electromagnetic pulse of wires in the wall, a noise so faint it's almost imaginary. Still, it's there, the modern world's replacement for running water. What's the difference between these grid noises—accomplices to our wired lives—and the sound of wind and moving water? Why does one feel like an intrusion and the other a lullaby?

"Too picky," Len has called me.

Perhaps.

I am certain of one thing, though. What matters and what is of little consequence becomes much clearer to me out there. In less quiet places, the noise surrounding my life disguises the difference.

Much as I don't want to, I feel myself changing shape as I lie in the clean bed—all the membranous parts of my exterior, having opened wide, refilling with the sounds of the wired planet. Tomorrow and the next day, I have that meeting. There will be eight, nine hours of talk in a closed room, the subject, ironically, being how to save America's vanishing wilderness. The climate control will be going in the background. I don't think about it. I think about the river—its moving water, its fish, its grizzlies, its birds, its constantly changing weather, and its old, old silence. Sitting up in bed, I switch on my headlamp and begin to write. Like most of us, ambivalent at coming back in, I search for a way to reconnect . . . to remember.

Acknowledgments

All quotes by John Franklin and John Richardson are from John Franklin, *Narrative of a Second Expedition to the Shores of the Polar Sea in the Years 1825, 1826, and 1827*, M. G. Hurtig Ltd., Edmonton, 1971.

All quotes by Vilhjalmur Stefansson are from Vilhjalmur Stefansson, *My Life with the Eskimo*, The Macmillan Company, New York, 1919. The quote from his diary is from June 9, 1912, and is cited in William R. Hunt, *Stef: A Biography of Vilhjalmur Stefansson*, University of British Columbia Press, Vancouver, 1986.

The quote by Edward Abbey is from Edward Abbey, *The Monkey Wrench Gang*, Avon Books, New York, 1975.

The quote by Erasmus Darwin is from Erasmus Darwin, Part II of *The Botanic Garden; A Poem in Two Parts. Part I. Containing the Economy of Vegetation. Part II. The Loves of the Plants with Philosophical Notes*, J. Johnson, London, 1791.

My discussion of the life cycles of mosquitoes, blackflies, and warble flies is indebted to E. C. Pielou, *A Naturalist's Guide to the Arctic*, The University of Chicago Press, Chicago, 1994.

My discussion of noise in industrial society equaling waste is indebted to Paul Hawken, Amory Lovins, and L. Hunter Lovins, *Natural Capitalism*, Little, Brown and Company, Boston, 1999.

I'm grateful for the editorial comments of Lorraine Bodger, Kim Fadiman, and Elizabeth Kaplan. I'm also thankful to Len's wife and my friend, Anne Ladd, for giving him the chance to go to the Arctic.